Suffering Is
Optional

The Myth of the Innocent Bystander

Morris L. Haimowitz, Ph.D., T.M.
Natalie R. Haimowitz, Ph.D., T.M.

ISBN No. 0-917790-01-4
Library of Congress Catalog Card No. 77-72839
1st Edition, 4th Printing

Dedicated to Our Students and Colleagues

ABOUT THE AUTHORS: Natalie Haimowitz, a clinical psychologist, has taught at Brooklyn College, Ohio State University and the University of Chicago. She was chief psychologist at Mary Thompson Women's and Children's Hospital, Chicago. Morris Haimowitz, a social psychologist, was Director, Human Relations Training, University of Chicago, Director of Human Relations, Chicago Public Schools, has taught at New York University, University of Wisconsin and Chicago City College. Their lectures, movies and television classes are known throughout the United States. They co-authored the book Human Development, now in its third edition which has been used by over 500 colleges and universities, and they have written many scientific articles. Both are Teaching Members and members of the Board of Trustees of the International Transactional Analysis Association. Morris and Natalie have been married 29 years, have three daughters, Carla, Myrna and Louise and are Co-Directors of Haimowoods Institute, a training center for professionals in social psychiatry.

Published by Haimowoods Press, 1101 Forest Ave., Evanston, IL 60202. Copyright © 1976 Morris L. Haimowitz, Ph.D. and Natalie R. Haimowitz, Ph.D. Typography by Optext Design Typography and Siemens Communication Graphics. Cover design by Myrna Haimowitz & Michael Waitsman. Mechanicals by Synthesis.

Acknowledgments

Most of the ideas in this book were learned from the members of the International Transactional Analysis Association. We are especially grateful to Eric Berne, who taught us over and over, and whose genius and friendship inspired us. We are grateful to our student colleagues. Many of the exercises they created are included.

How can we acknowledge the hundreds of people who have taught us in workshops, classes, books and articles? Dr. Fritz Perls, who showed us how to be free while freeing others. Dr. Carl Rogers, who taught us to listen. Dr. Sigmund Freud, who demonstrated humility with genius. Dr. Bob Goulding and Mary Goulding, and David Kupfer who came to us and permitted us to go to them, and to Claude Steiner for the stroke economy and script matrix.

The great contributions of Alfred Adler must be noted. Seventy years ago he was giving the world inside glimpses of strange human behavior, writing eloquently of games people played to get attention, even negative attention, and how people pretended to be sick, stupid, clumsy or crazy to get their way. Adler created the idea that each child decided his unique lifestyle which now we call *Script*, and Adler showed how understanding his fairy tale helped the therapist understand the patient.

We are grateful for the able assistance of Carla Haimowitz who not only transcribed the original document but also dialogued with us frequently to influence our thinking. Thanks, also to Gail Stall and especially to Dolores Carlin who typed and typed as we changed and changed. We are enriched by their advice, patience and sensitivity.

We are pleased to acknowledge the help of Elaine Kittredge and Fred Hallanger in the preparation of this manuscript.

Table of Contents

I. Introduction

Transactional analysis is the study of the ways in which people get stuck in certain ways of feeling and behaving by the accident of the particular kind of early experiences they have had and how they stay stuck in these, playing games to confirm that's how the world was when they were little and how it is still good, bad, or indifferent. It's incredible that if people were rough and harsh with you when you were a kid, some part of you still puts energy into looking for people who are apt to act rough and mean to you. In some way you let people know you expect them to be rough and cruel to you. You probably make it easy for them to be rough with you, and you may even bully the people around you into being rough and cruel to you.

Transactional analysis is a system of social psychiatry and psychotherapy unique in its use of simple language and treatment contracts.

No theory of human behavior or system of psychotherapy springs fullblown as a totally new innovation independent of what has preceded. Inventions occur as an outgrowth of current knowledge, existing beliefs and practices.

Psychiatrist Eric Berne invented TA in 1956 after studying to be a psychoanalyst for twelve years. Psychoanalysis had been the most important body of theory and practice since 1900, so that we may consider transactional analysis to be an outgrowth of Freudian psychology. Therapists were familiar with dynamic psychiatry. Also, by the time Berne was creating transactional analysis, Carl Rogers already had been treating the patient while he or she* was sitting up, listening to him, understanding his feelings without interpreting them, and respecting the patient's decision about what he wanted to change. (Rogers referred to counselees as "clients" rather than as patients, an expression of his approach which saw people as equal and healthy rather than inferior and sick.)

Alfred Adler, a student of Freud, had already advanced his theories of life style and how these are formed in early years. Adlerians were already working with families and with groups of people in community clinics.

Lee Bradford and his band of social psychologists interested in group dynamics were already using T groups and describing predictable, repetitive, frustrating interpersonal "games" which were being played out in groups.

Fritz Perls, the psychoanalyst who formed the Gestalt School, had already

---

*In order to give equal time to "he" and "she," we will use these pronouns alternately, so that usually he means he or she, and she means she or he.

developed concepts such as unfinished business, the "top dog" (public) self and the "underdog" (private) self, the "now," dreamwork without interpretation, the concept of the experiment. Jacob Moreno had discovered a better way to work with dreams and fantasies than by talking about them, and in his institute in Beacon, N.Y. had developed a major contribution—psychodrama. Those interested in behavior modification had already begun to study how and when stroking may be effective in changing behavior. TA is used by thousands of people who have many different ideas about what it is. This is our version of some of the TA concepts. We have not included all. Rather we are allowing ourselves the freedom to tell about those ideas which interest us most. Also, we will describe what we believe now. What we believe now and what we do is very different from what we believed five years ago, and what we used to do then. And what we present here may be different from what we do and believe five years from now.

A note on pain

This book is about pain, some caused by feelings, memories or behavior, some physically caused in the form of accidents, cancer, heart disease, arthritis, tobacco, drug or other pollutants. A good deal of physical pain can be prevented or reduced by a way of life which includes exercise, rest, fun, good food, love, contact, responding to others, and being responded to by people, animals, plants.

For most of the people reading this book whose suffering is optional, we have good news. This kind of chronic state of misery may be alleviated or eliminated. For many people who are victimized, suffering is not optional. Today hundreds of millions of people are existing on the verge of starvation. Millions are being tortured or harassed for racial, political or religious beliefs. All over this planet ten million refugees suffer without a country, the cup of their culture broken. For them suffering may not be optional.

On the other hand, many of us hurt ourselves in exquisitely creative ways. We may have learned in childhood that pain brought delicious sympathy. So we may hurt ourselves by disregarding good judgement: use tobacco, alcohol or drugs; eat foods with too much fat, sugar or salt, avoid vegetables, fruits and whole grains; disregard what we know about the consequences of not exercising or resting appropriately, by thinking thoughts that make us sad, scared or angry; by obsessing about old hurts and resentments; by not being responsible caring citizens in a society which sorely needs participation in the nurturing of its children, old folks, and disadvantaged; by not helping to insure clean air, clean water, clean government and good schools; and by relying on others to assess our needs and also to shape the means to achieve them; i.e. to set things up for us like mommy and daddy did.

2

II. Strokes

A stroke is any response or recognition that you exist. Getting response is essential to life. If children do not get response from others, they die. Experiments with many mammals—rats, monkeys, pigs, goats, sheep, dogs—show that if the newborn receives no strokes, even though he is warm and has food, he will become very sick or die. Human infants also died at a high rate in orphan asylums where they were kept clean and warm and fed because there were not enough adults to give the infants adequate stimulation. This changed dramatically when orphans were placed in foster homes, even without especially loving foster parents, because there were more strokes in foster homes than in asylums.

Around 1930, the people who were interested in child-placement discovered that children did much better even in dirty, abusive foster homes than in clean, indifferent orphan asylums. What they discovered is that there is another dimension to child-rearing besides food, clothing and shelter, and that dimension is stroking, touching, response. A child needs to be touched, patted, bounced up and down, talked to, in order for his brain and muscles to develop and to breathe evenly. As a baby, stroking is literally touching. Later on, just a wink will do or a nod or a smile from Mommy. When we get older and are capable of symbolic behavior, a word, a letter, a gold star, a merit award are strokes. "Hello" is a stroke. Someone saying my name out loud is a stroke. From a celebrity or a sweetheart, it may be worth one hundred strokes. Sometimes the recognition is a bawling out or a beating. A kick is a stroke, too, and if a boy has survival in mind, a kick is much better than nothing at all. Children who are beaten survive; children who are ignored (*i.e.* not stroked) die. We are not suggesting that anyone should go around beating kids; we are saying that people need to know that stroking is essential, that children and grown-ups need to be touched. If they cannot get tender loving strokes, and do get kicked, kicks will keep them alive.

It is helpful to identify four kinds of strokes. Early in life people get addicted to one of the four kinds, defining the particular kind they like as a necessity and seeking that particular kind of stroke in their involvements with others.

The four kinds of strokes are as follows: (1) positive strokes (+) which feel good and say you're O.K. ("warm fuzzies"), like being smiled at, hugged, admired, or chosen for something good; (2) negative strokes (−) which feel bad and say you're not O.K. ("cold pricklies"), like being spanked, criticized, put down, snubbed, or sent to bed without supper. In addition to warm fuzzies and cold pricklies, there are two other varieties, (3) warm pricklies (+ −) and (4) cold fuzzies (− +), both of which are pleasure and love offered in combination with pain and degradation. "Hi, you loveable ding-bat," is a warm pricklie, as is, "Well, how nice! You finally combed your hair!" A cold fuzzie is the giving of a treat in the attitude of anger and resentment. Willie wants 25¢ to get a toy, and his mother throws the quarter at him with an attitude of "Take it, you rotten lousy kid," which makes getting the treat a bittersweet experience. Children need strokes to survive and will die without them. And although children thrive best on positive strokes, negative strokes will keep a child alive, as well as the mixed varieties.

People who are used to positive strokes, who expect positive strokes and seek them out usually do not come for psychotherapy. What we find is that people go through life seeking the very same kind they received as children. For example, if when a little girl asked for something she got a response like, "Take the cookie and choke!" which is a gift combined with anger and hatred, she pursues responses of begrudging generosity later on in her life. Some people have learned to live on + −. They are unmoved by a simple positive stroke or somehow convert it into a cold fuzzy in their heads (i.e., "They gave me what I wanted just to shut me up or get rid of me."). Others like warm fuzzies. Give them a smile and their headache disappears and they feel good. Given a + − they salvage the + part and somehow use it. ("If she took the time to call me up and chew me out, I sure must be important to her.").

Some people accustomed in childhood to getting kicks pursue them later in life. Give them a kick and that will be the big event of the week. They will tell 25 people "So and so called me a liar!" and will brood about it! But if you tell them "I like you," they may not even hear it, or may convert it into a kick ("He was just being patronizing."). If a person needs air, bad air may be better than no air at all.

Warm Pricklies & Cold Fuzzies

Listed below are some common examples of warm pricklies and cold fuzzies.

Warm pricklies: (+ −) a kick given in a nice way.
>   a big hug, which leaves you with a broken rib or a sore kidney
>   pinching a child's cheek very hard while uttering words of endearment
>   a warm handshake which leaves your hand hurting
>   "I see you're on time!"
>   "Great! You finally paid your bill."
>   "You look much better since you lost 20 pounds."
>   "Isn't Johnny nice! He didn't wet his pants today."
>   "What did you do to yourself. You really look good."
>   "What are *you* doing here?"
>   "When are you leaving?"
>   Making love and discovering you have contracted V.D.

Cold fuzzies: (− +) a goodie given in a negative way.
>   "Take the cookie (and choke)."
>   "You can have it!" (throws it on floor).
>   "Take the money!" (throws it on floor).
>   "Take the car. I'll be all right. I can walk (I'll suffer)."

4

"Go to the party. I'll manage (I'll punish you by pouting)."

"So get married, and leave me (you're crummy like all the rest)."

"Have a good time. Don't worry about me. (I'll agree to your going if you promise to feel guilty)."

"O.K., hurry up. I'm in a hurry; tell me what you want to tell me and get it over with (you're a burden)."

"You took my chair. It's O.K. (what can I expect from a selfish oaf like you?)."

Berne felt that the child at birth was born a prince or princess, feeling very good about herself and others; but some children were turned into "frogs" by "frog-parents" who offered mainly love mixed with pain. and humiliation, or stroked for the child's behaving in a not O.K. fashion and for the child's feeling not O.K. Here are examples.

Some Special Ways of Adapting for Strokes

The Sulk: Alone, sad, and angry, she lives with the feeling that she is deserted and silently and sullenly she sits in a suit of armor, and once a month opens the visor, looks around, and says "Go to Hell!" and slams the visor shut. Sadness and crankiness are visible on her face, but she refuses to say what she wants, so people who care about her or need affection from her try to guess. Rescuers attempt to draw the Sulk into their activities: "Come on Sally, take an apple, or come swimming with us, or give us a tiny smile." Other people go away. Many Sulks secretly feel very powerful, withdraw and hold back, living as though, if they expressed their feelings, they might hurt someone. Often the feeling of being deserted began at age four when parents were divorced or grandma died, or a baby brother was born, or her dog was run over. What keeps the system going is that other people keep "feeding" it, stroking Sally when she is sad by taking on themselves Sally's job of figuring out what Sally wants, *i.e.* making a tremendous energy investment in Sally, stroking her more when she is sad and sulky.

The Jerk: Tries to help, but invariably screws up; plays such games as Why does it always happen to me?, I'm only trying to help, kick me, yes-but, creditor, schlemiel, wooden leg, stupid, confused, and harried. If, in a treatment group the therapist or facilitator asks the Jerk to get some strokes, the Jerk will usually ask the group Sulk, a person that everyone knows doesn't give strokes. We speculate that the Jerk learned this style at around age two or three when he was given jobs he couldn't quite do by a helpless parent who wanted him to grow up fast, or by a competitive parent who wanted to look better than the child. He still spills the soup or hurries to come late.

The Prick: A show-off, doing better than anyone else, the Prick is often rescuing others and getting the praise when things turn out well and the blame when things turn out badly. The Prick hogs the strokes and lives an active, initiating, "I'll do it!" life. At age four, she was already running the family, the first to wash the dishes. Her mother said, "What shall I wear tonight, Sweety?" and the Prick knew the right thing to wear. She believes "If I take care of my mother, she will take care of me." When we ask a class of students, "Where could I find some chalk?" the Prick jumps up, runs out of the room, and brings us some, thereby

5

outdoing all the others who just sat.

Thus, a person's definite, repetitive, consistent behavior patterns probably originated in the stroking patterns of her parents. We may imagine her as a small child getting great approval or disapproval—but certainly getting strokes from parents for whatever particular kind of behavior is now repetitive. The Prick plays such games as Look ma, no hands, picture picture on the wall and Miss America. She gets the blue ribbon for the best apple pie, and is probably in *Who's Who*. Pricks do more than their share of the work and get much praise, but they often feel depressed and angry because "if I take care of you, you will take care of me" isn't true in their lives. Pricks work harder than their fellows and feel cheated.

The Way It Was

Few people are 100% Sulks or Jerks or Pricks. Lots of people are agile enough to switch from one of these positions to another. For example, a woman gets a divorce to marry her lover, and then finds her lover won't divorce his wife, will probably insist that she is surprised at the turn of events and had no idea that in the end she would be the "spare" or extra woman in her lover's life. She has probably set it up to be number two or second best. We find that as a child she also was second best with her father who flirted with her but always went back to her mother. Her lover, who has it set up to have a wife as well as a mistress—without being very close to either—as a child, went from his grandmother to his mother and back to grandmother, both of whom competed for his control and affection, and both of whom gave extra bonus strokes for his attention because of the competition. So years later he sets up relationships in which people are having a tug of war over him. He experiences repeatedly the added importance he has to both, the extra strokes he gets in this position, but also the extra stress and discomfort.

The point is that many people have arranged their lives as adults to duplicate many of the very same stroke arrangements they experienced as children. In some uncanny way, those of us who were bullied as children often have within our grown-up selves a Child who continues to subtly but relentlessly invite bullying from others, and we keep this operation secret from ourselves so that we feel "done in" by others, unaware of the part we ourselves play in the repetition. So people who are hooked into self-destructive patterns learned as infants that the only way to survive was to get kicks, criticism, abuse from their parents, and they become expert in getting people to kick them. Here they are twenty, forty, or fifty years later and they're still stuck, expecting only kicks, failures, criticism, negative strokes, and specializing in how to bug people in order to get those kicks. They don't need the kicks now to survive, but continue to act as though they do.

I'm Looking for Kicks

Some people are in the cold prickly business. They have antennas going, click, click, click, and if there is an insult to be gotten somewhere in the room, they receive it. They are easily offended (in the negative-stroke business). When people say something nice to them, they shrug it off. It doesn't count. They are only on the lookout for insults, hurts, and abuses.

What Turns You On?

The behavior modification people have conducted thousands of experiments to show how strokes change behavior. Here is one example that was done by a psychologist named Verplank. If we were conducting this experiment, we would proceed as follows. I would ask you to name as many nouns as you could out loud. Now if you are a good guy and oblige and say, perhaps, "mat, table, chair, picture..." and so on, and if every time you say a plural, "apples, thighs..." I would very quietly say, "hmmm," inside of ten minutes, you are saying many more plurals than before without even knowing it. Now, if I knew I was turned on by plurals, that would really be something, because I could get everyone into saying plurals with some well-placed "hmmm's." Suppose it's sexy talk I'm turned on by. Then (with my quiet little "hmmm") I could get people talking sexy. If aggression excites me, every time you say something aggressive, I say "hmmm." Inside of a short time, you're really doing it. Now if I know I'm doing that with you, that's pretty sharp. But suppose I don't even know. Suppose I don't know I get excited by plurals, but I'm training everyone around me to say plurals all the time, and every time they do I stroke them for it. Suppose you're my little boy and you need strokes to survive, and if every time you say a plural I stroke you, your number of plurals is going to increase because that's what's going to keep you alive. That's how children get hooked into their parents' games. If I'm turned on by X and you're my kid, and I'm the one person in the world who will stroke you, you start Xing all over the place. If the X happens to be your vomiting and being sick so I can have someone to take care of, you're going to be sick. If it happens to be your breaking windows, then you will break windows. This is extremely important. This is a crucial issue in how people learn to be sick, to vomit, to cry, to be happy, to wheeze, sneeze, act crazy or whatever. When people know they need strokes and they're going to trade something for them, then they're in a better position to take care of themselves.

Easy ways to get strokes: ask for one, wink, wave, say "hello," wear funny socks or scarves. Hard ways to get strokes: make a million dollars, go crazy, have asthma, colitis, heart attack or depression, become president.

The Need for Excitement

Sometimes a little boy gets the message that he is expected to break windows at school. For any number of reasons, his mother or father needs him to do it. Let's make it a simple reason. Every person has an animal body, has a pituitary gland, an adrenal gland, a liver, and blood vessels which need to be excited every once in a while, the heart needs to go faster every now and again, and let's say that this may be a physiological need. That is, one of the theories is that there is a need to be homeostatic, that is to be stable. We're saying there is also a different need, and that is to be unstable. In other words, people need to be excited every once in a while, and to our knowledge, there is little about this in any of the literature—not even in the TA literature. So, let's say the mother needs some excitement. Her work and her husband have been routine, dull, maybe boring. The safest, most exciting event for her would be for her kid to break into some house or be sick, to vomit, to have asthma or to have cancer. Any one of these things would get her really excited. Her kid could be a good dancer or "a brain." "Oh, he dances beautifully!" When he dances, she gets really excited.

All animals need some excitement—this seems to be a physiological, a biological need. We all need stimulation. The evidence is that everybody does this, one way or another. When they don't do it, they get bored and start to do some things that get them excited. They may become depressed or they may become happy. They may go out and dance or sing or have sex or rob a bank. You could go to the movies; that might be exciting enough for you. The person next to you might need to play Russian roulette. Just what you choose for excitement has to do with what we are talking about.

Legends and Self Stroking

You have a legend, your reputation (*i.e.*, what you were famous for in your family). Your mother probably told everybody that Victor was X. Smart: "He's my smart son." Reliable: "That's my reliable son." Or, "That's my brave boy . . . or the shy one" Or, "That's my fuck-up kid. He sure screws up everything." Or, "That's my difficult one," or "That's my sick one." Or, "He's the family artist" or "the family liar." Everybody has a legend, and that's what your mother or your family expects you to be. Mom will tell you stories about how you were that way before you even could remember. "Victor, before you could remember, you were so good I didn't know there was a kid in the house." Her message is: "You damn sure better not ask for anything!" or "You're the kind of kid who's supposed to get along on nothing. If everyone else needs a meal, you could make it on a peanut. Don't ask." Victor learns to be good and get his excitement in his dreams. So, later on, people stroke themselves for what their parents stroked them for. If mother stroked you every time you suffered, later on you stroke yourself every time you suffer. And the problem is that people then become their own "hmmm," they incorporate the Parent (develop a part of themselves just like their own parents) to stroke themselves in ways that might even be destructive to their own Kid. If a mother stroked us for it, we do it—so people starve themselves or eat too much, or go to prison, or do all sorts of things that are destructive because that is how they got strokes from Mommy or Daddy when they were two or three.

Being a kid is like being stuck in a dungeon with two giants because you can't go shopping for parents when you're six months old. You're stuck. You can't decide when you are one year old whom you will have supper with. The problem of early childhood is figuring out those two giants. That's everybody's problem the first year of life; how to make it with those big shots. If Mommy and Daddy come to see you once a day with a cup of milk and say, "Now we're going to give you a chance to do something to please us." "Oh? Sorry about that, sonny, we'll be back tomorrow night with the milk, since you didn't please us tonight." Then you figure out how to please them, baby, because you need that milk to survive. By milk, we mean strokes. Parents tell their kids, "This is the way it is everywhere," or "Don't you take milk from anybody else. If you think it's easy to get milk out there, well, that's all poison. The only one you can take milk from is me." And we see people, thirty, forty, fifty years old, who are hooked into self-destructive scripts, but they also got messages, "Don't listen to anybody else." So then the person himself begins to self-stroke the way mother and father stroked. Whether a person's self-stroking is a comforting thing or a harsh thing gives you some clue as to how he was stroked. Some people say to themselves like the Little Train that Could: "I know I can, I know I can..." while other people say to themselves, "You jerk, you've gone and screwed it up again." And some even slap themselves on the hands, legs, or face as they call themselves "stupid," "nasty," "selfish," or the other terms stated verbally or implied by their real parents.

As we mentioned earlier, there are four kinds of strokes. We call the positive strokes warm fuzzies: hugs or kisses, or "I like you." And the negative strokes would be kicks or "I hate you," or "Get out of here," or "Drop dead," or "You're all wrong"; and the mixed kind of strokes which feature love and joy mixed with pain and humiliation. Some people go through life picking up warm fuzzies all the time. If somebody says one bad thing to them and one good thing, they'll remember the one good thing. They're picking up warm fuzzies and they're feeling good most of the time. Other people go through life picking up the cold pricklies. If someone says a hundred good things to them and one bad thing, they will believe and remember the one bad thing. They feel bad most of the time. Then there's "sweet-sour" stroke collectors. They collect warm pricklies and usually turn down warm fuzzies as "insincere" or "effusive." All games involve a warm prickly. For example, someone says, "Come here, let me hug you." You go to them and they squeeze you until your ribs break. Or they shake hands so hard your fingers go limp. You've seen adults pinch the cheeks of children until it hurts. If a child learns that love hurts, he looks for somebody in the world to both love and hurt him at the same time. By stroking, parents teach a kid what kind of stroke he is supposed to get, whether it's positive or negative or sweet-sour, how much he needs, and how to get it in the world. In some families, hypochondria is rewarded. In others, you get noticed if you are depressed. In still others, achievement is rewarded. And in some families, it doesn't matter if you get a good mark, it only counts if you're the best. If Mommy's into competing with her brother, and her little Willy comes home with all A's, Mommy says, "How many others had all A's?" "Oh, no others, Wonderful, Willy!" "Oh, five others had all A's...well, that's O.K. Do better next time." Parents stroke kids for living out the parents' dreams, fears, obsessions or unexpressed rebellions.

In some families the message is, "You are never satisfied." For example, parents encourage the child's appetite for goodies or for being "center stage" and then they zap him for showing off too much. Mommy urges the little boy to perform for relatives and friends. "Show the company how nicely you play the piano," she might say (show off for me), or even urge him non-verbally by laughing at his antics, and then suddenly, when she grows weary of him, want him to go to bed. When he seems resistive, she says, "You never have enough. Give a pig a finger and he wants a whole hand!" Or Mommy gives the kid something—an infrequent hug—and the kid wants another hug. Mommy doesn't say, "I'm bored with you," or "I'm impatient," or "I'm afraid to get close." Instead, she says, "You never have enough." She doesn't tell the child about herself, she tells him he's not O.K. She doesn't say, "I'm O.K., you're O.K." She says, "The trouble around here is that you never have enough." Then the child runs around feeling "Something's wrong with me; I can never be satisfied." He grabs all the food, or all the strokes in the room; he has to be first; he snatches what he wants and runs. He can be openly greedy because his mother told him, "You're never satisfied." This is how he lives out the prophecy.

In some families, Mommy is very guilt-ridden, but impulsive, so if the kid is annoying, she socks the kid and then she feels guilty and says, "I'm sorry." Hug, hug, hug, kiss, kiss, kiss, cookie, cookie, cookie, and the kid says, "Gee, in this world you've first got to get kicked before you get kissed. That's the way to make it. So if I make people mad at me, then they're going to make love to me." Such people are very provocative—provocative with their husbands, wives and children, because in their heads the stroking pattern is that you have to get kicked before you get kissed.

I'm O.K.; You're O.K.

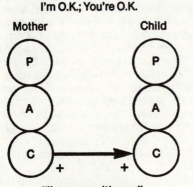

"I'm angry with you."
"I'm impatient."
"I'm afraid to get close."
"I'm bored."
"I don't know what to do."
"I'm sorry I can't give you better food, we have no money."
"I like you, let's play."

I'm O.K.; You're Not O.K.

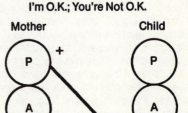

"Don't bother me."
"Go practice the piano."
"Stand up straight."
"You are never satisfied."
"What's wrong with you?"
"You're always complaining."

III. Structure of Personality

Berne recognized three major structural components of the person: the Child, the Adult, and the Parent. At any moment in time, a person is in one of the three ego states. People change ego states at will and a person may flip, for example, from being in a Child ego state to being in her Adult or Parent. Unlike other theories, TA theory is written in simple language so that it can be understood by an eight-year-old. We insist on this because the Child part of each person has a great deal of the person's power and energy. In fact, the Child is in control, running the show, and can know what's going on if the words are clear.

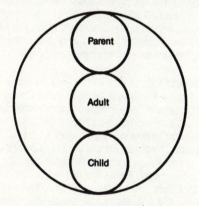

Structure of a Person. Each person has three perfect parts or ego states. Capital letters are used to express ego states. Lower case letters are used to express real people: parent (mother or dad), child (son or daughter).

The Child Ego State

At birth the Natural Child can do many things. She can kick, suck, burp, urinate, and eliminate. She likes to be rocked, fed, talked to, held. Most of her cells know what to do and how to react under varying circumstances. The baby cries when she feels uncomfortable, heedless of whether she is in a private place like home or in a public place like the movies or an airplane. The baby mainly is in touch with her senses and protests loudly if she feels bad. We call this part of the person the Free Child. When the baby cries, it's a signal that she wants to get fed or rocked or changed.

At first the Natural Child is not in touch with the world outside her skin except as it impinges on her, that is, something feels too hot or someone is handling her roughly or kochee-kooing her. Almost any observer living anywhere in the world can see almost any baby and very accurately determine whether the baby is content, at ease, slightly distressed, very uncomfortable, or in extreme pain. The infant hasn't yet learned the subtleties of social living, that is, what to hide of her natural reactivity. Just before Mom feeds her, changes her, or picks her up, Mommy might say, "Hey, I'm coming!" or "Don't cry. Mommy is on the way," or "Shut up already!"

There is a very acute intelligence in the young child soon after birth—and for all of his life, if he uses it. It is an intelligence based on sensations rather than language or logical thinking. Very soon after birth, the hungry baby reacts to the noise in the kitchen as well as to the discomfort in his stomach. Many babies stop crying when Mommy comes, even before being fed. We call this part of the Child the Little Professor. It's the part of the Child that somehow senses what's going on, that is, Mommy and Daddy are having a party tonight and I think I'll stay awake, or, the lady standing there is not a visitor but a baby-sitter and Mommy is about to leave. The Little Professor is the part of the Child that begins to cry as soon as he gets into the doctor's office knowing somehow that it is shot-time-minus-ten-minutes.

After a few months (and for the rest of her life) the baby learns that there are official and unofficial rules that must be followed in order to "make it" in the world. ("In the world" means in her particular family.) Don't bite Mommy's nipple. Don't spit up on Mommy's new dress. You have to yell your head off before others respond. Show off. Or don't show off. Be clumsy so Dad can look agile. Be sick so Mommy can take care of you. Be stupid so your parents won't be afraid you'll gab about their big secrets: Dad was arrested for cheating on his income tax; Mom "turns on" with the roofer. These are not verbalized, and often the parents are not even aware that they want their children to behave in these ways. Messages are expressed by the parents not so much with direct orders, but rather with smiles or scowls, by giving pats and nods, or by withholding affection or turning their backs or walking away. Many of these messages (we call them "injunctions") or no-no's are given before the child learns spoken language.

For Freud, the id was a mass of insatiable drives, hungers, lusts, aggressions, angers, curiosity. For TA, each child is satiable. If she is hungry, she gets her milk and is satisfied; or, if she wants to be rocked a few minutes, her mother or father rocks her and she is satisfied. If the mother resents the amount of care a child requires, and says, "This baby wants too much of me. She is never satisfied," it is very likely that the girl comes to think of herself as never satisfied and arranges to be that way. Many times later in life, she will again turn on this dissatisfied two-year-old Child in herself and feel and act like a "difficult" spoiled brat who is unsatisfiable.

12

Adapting for Survival: The Adapted Child

Soon after birth, the child must not only get someone to take care of him (feed, dress, protect him from injury), but the baby also has to get strokes (be touched, talked to, listened to, smiled at). If the infant isn't taken care of physically and also stroked, he becomes very ill and may die. Some parents stroke their child (that is, come look at him, touch the baby, feed him, "turn on") when he cries; others ignore the baby when the baby cries, but stroke him when he smiles; and some stroke when the child sneezes or wheezes; others stroke for achievement; some parents stroke generously for sickness. Thus, some children learn to get from their parents the strokes they need to survive by playing helpless, stupid, or confused; others survive by being bright, organized go-getters; still others learn that their parents are excited when they are a bully, or a "crybaby." Even as plants grow toward light, so children learn whatever forms of behavior their parents or their caretakers stroke. Parents are aware of many of the things that excite them, but unaware of others. This is why many children behave in ways that pain and perplex parents who are unaware of much about themselves and not in touch with how they have "turned on" to the child's "undesirable" behaviors. We are not implying that parents necessarily "like" the undesired behavior, but rather that they "turn on," get excited by, or respond with more energy to the "undesired" behavior.

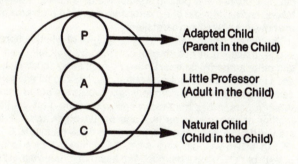

Structure of the Child Ego State

The Adapted Child, then, is a free spirit who has become trained to act in a special way because he needs strokes to stay alive. In his family, he gets strokes for being very smart or very stupid, generous or stingy, fast or slow, nervous or calm, whiney, afraid or fearless, miserable when alone or miserable with other people, clumsy or agile, helpless or independent, vague or precise, clean or messy, prompt or late, long-suffering martyr or bully, or like any of the Seven Dwarfs: Happy, Sleepy, Dopey, Grumpy, Sneezy, Doc, Bashful. The Adapted Child may act stupid, with toe scuffling on the floor, shoulders up to his ears, while he says "I dunno"—or he may be the first to be helpful when I ask for some chalk, or very stubborn in resisting a command, or shy with people.

The Parent Ego State

Even before the youngster begins to speak at about the age of one year, and from then on, the parents verbalize rules. Do your BM in the toilet, not in your pants; don't stick your finger in the electric plug; stay with Mommy and Daddy; don't make noise here. Then later: don't go out with "loose" girls; don't get in debt; don't pick up your baby when he cries or you will spoil him. We call these spoken rules (the "should's" and "ought's" of life) the Parent part of the person. The infant literally learns to imitate and repeat the do's and don'ts of his parents with their affect, in their words and with their posture. This becomes part of his Child ego state, an adaptation to the caretakers, in which he imitates them to keep himself in line. We call this the Parent in the Child (or P_1). When a small child has his Parent on (P_1), he sounds like a kid playing dress-up, like a caricature of a bossy Marine sergeant or some other highly stereotyped caricature of the grown-ups around him.

Later on in life (sometime between the ages of 5 and 30, another Parent ego state (called P_2) is gradually formed, usually as a result of a whole series of testy clashes, pushes and pulling against the caretakers, observing a variety of caretakers, and having lots of experiences in solving problems and finding out about the how-to's of life from caretakers.

The Parent (P_2) is thus a living catalogue of what's supposed to be right and wrong, usually (but not always) obtained by watching and listening to parents and other authority figures. Unlike Freud's superego, which is a system of rules and concepts, the Parent ego state in transactional analysis is made up of real parents whose actions, emotions, and words are acted out right in front of one. When a person has his Parent ego state turned on, he literally looks like his mother or father, sounds like one or the other, takes the same posture and stance, literally becomes that person for a few moments. One can see the Parent (P_1) in a two-year-old who says, "You mustn't drop candy wrappers in the street" or "You need a haircut." I've heard my three-year-old scold: "What kind of mother are you?" In the film *The Yellow Submarine,* the Parent was dramatically portrayed by a glove that would go "Zap!" and people would turn into stone. When a person is pointing an accusing or assertive finger, this is often a clue that his Parent ego state is on.

The Parent uses a wide variety of words. *You* is often a parent word. If a person is talking about herself and says "you" meaning "I" ("You can't expect people to keep secrets if you can't keep them yourself.")—at that moment, she is playing a Parent tape in her head. Wilder Penfield has conducted experiments in which the brain was exposed and the experimenter touched the brain with an electrode. When the brain is stimulated in a certain spot, the person remembers something. The person says, "Yes, I am remembering being..." She recalls the event and the feelings she had then, and if the electrode is touched to the brain at another spot, the person remembers something very different, an event perhaps thirty years before the first memory. Every experience is recorded in the brain as though on a tape recorder and remains there for life. When the mother says to her daughter, "You can't trust men," we know that the mother is probably playing an old Parent tape in her head. She becomes her mother telling her, "You can't trust men." In this way bits of misinformation may be passed down from generation to generation.

Here is a little boy. His Mommy is big and she is saying, "You should brush your teeth." The word *you* is a clue that the Parent ego state is on. *You should* with a pointed finger is characteristic behavior of someone in a Parent ego state. *You should, you ought, you must,* are good clues. So the Parent is the person's guide, implanted in his head to direct him long after his parents are gone. The rules about how to get along in the world in Mommy and Daddy's voice, with their gestures and feelings, are part of him forever, *a role that he himself turns on.* * Stop at a red light; look before you cross the street; eat everything on your plate; don't eat too much; this is the way to wash your clothes." Some of these rules are helpful ("Be who you are; respect yourself and others; eat well; exercise; rest and have fun"), some are burdens ("Eat your spinach; be nice to everyone; get everyone to like you; anything worth doing is worth doing well; always be good; never borrow money; always tell the truth; early to bed..."), and some are just plain harmful ("Never cry; finish everything you start; be the best; never come in second; be perfect; hurry up; don't let people know what you are feeling..."). Words that imply judgment of ethics or value are also usually parental: stupid; lazy; good boy; honest; hostile; kind; obedient; willful; arrogant; generous. And when a person starts using some fancy, sophisticated words such as: improper; appropriate; achievement; responsibility; democracy; one knows that the person is probably in his attempting-to-be-important Parent ego state. The Natural Child speaks with simple words.

Another clue that someone has her Parent on is the situation. The Parent helps the child. There are two kinds of Parent ego states: the Nurturing Parent and the Critical Parent. The Nurturing Parent nurtures and cares for the child, feeds, warms, bathes, holds, rocks her, sings sweet songs, reads stories, says "I love you." When a person has her Nurturing Parent on, she is probably taking care of herself or others. The Critical Parent fills the child with rules about living in the outside world: "Always come on time." "Pay attention." "Think before you act." "Always tell the truth." "Don't speak to strangers." "Look at me when I'm talking to you." "Men don't cry." "Vote this way, don't vote that way." "Black people are good—white people are bad." "Don't play with those children." Any kinds of rules about society come from the Critical Parent. We're not saying that the Nurturing Parent is good and the Critical Parent is bad; we're saying that these are two aspects of the Parent. For example, the Nurturing Parent may nurture the kid to death, keep stuffing her with food, sleep with baby until she's twenty-five,

*This is an important idea. Often people prefer to believe that things "happen" in their heads over which they have no control. Once a person acknowledges that he activates whatever goes on in his head, he is on his way to changing his life.

make all her important decisions—overnurture, in other words. The Critical Parent may be helpful; there are important rules the child needs to know about society to protect herself. "Cross the street between the lines." "Wait for the green light." "Don't drink anything from a bottle that has a skull and crossbones on it." "Don't play in the street." The Critical Parent may also be bigoted and warn the child against dangers which do not exist. She thus may hurt the child by telling her lies that limit her unnecessarily and deprive her of adventures and experiments and strokes. "Black people are bad." "Don't play with boys." "Don't talk to strangers." "Stay home, Columbus, the earth is flat." So that Nurturing Parent and Critical Parent refer to different functions, both aimed at helping the child to survive when the real parent is no longer there to supervise or help. Very often, a person turns on her Parent ego state when her Child is afraid. The Child, scared of danger or criticism, cries "Help!" and her own Parent comes on to rescue.

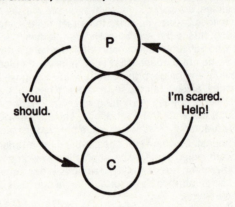

The Adult Ego State

The child begins to develop an Adult ego state when he knows the bottle or breast is "not me." I am I and Mommy is Mommy. During the first year, he begins to crawl, to touch and taste many new objects and in the second year, two other great developments take place: the child learns to speak and walk. The young child can now get around by himself (crawling or walking) and is less and less restricted to being only where people carry him. Also, the child is mastering words, thereby acquiring a great filing system for information with other people. The Adult is that part of the person which takes in information and computes probabilities. The Adult is a computer which acknowledges and stores information about the insides of the person and about the outside world, and solves problems.

The Adult is the least exciting of the three ego states, although the solutions to problems solved by the Adult may be very exciting. When a person has her Adult turned on, she is without feeling and lacking the dramatic expressiveness

16

of the Child or the Parent: This is a 9 x 12 rug and you are people and I am here and you have a red shirt on. The Adult perceives what is going on in the present in the world by using the five senses, and it also has access to information acquired in the past (memory). My Adult may tell me, "If I steal, I stand a 50-50 chance of getting into trouble." "If I pay for what I take, I stand zero chance of getting into trouble." So the Adult is computing the possibilities and probabilities of various opportunities. The Adult is an extremely important part of the person, but it is not creative, exuberant, or spontaneous like the Child or nurturing or full of rules like the Parent. The Adult voice is a matter-of-fact voice. The Critical Parent and the Adult may sometimes agree. Lots of things your parents told you turn out to be true: "Don't touch the fire." That's why you survived. If too much of what they told you were not true, and you weren't allowed to check it out, you would be dead or in serious trouble. Many people don't check out or verify their prejudices to see if they are really true. Is it really true that if I step on a crack I will break my mother's back? If the Critical Parent gives the child crazy rules and then says she mustn't check them out, then the kid is in trouble. Some parents are hurt when children "check out" Parent input. The parents say, "You are bad," or "You are wild," or "God will punish you." "If you loved me you would do as I say." Other parents encourage testing out. "Find out for yourself," they say. Such children have permission to use their Adult. One of the differences between TA and psychoanalysis is that psychoanalysts say there is such a thing as a weak ego. In TA there is no such thing as a weak Adult among ordinary persons. Every person has an Adult. Some people turn it on more than others. There are ways to engage the Adult. For example, "What day is today?" ("Tuesday.") "How many fingers do you have on your right hand?" ("Five.") "Tell me what you see." ("I see the yellow rose.") "What rhymes with rose?" ("Toes.")

Identifying Ego States

When we speak to someone, that person may be in his Parent ego state or in his Adult or in his Child. It is very important for you to know which ego state he is in if you wish to influence him, because he reacts very differently to the same comment when his Child is turned on than when he is living in his Adult or Parent.

There are many behaviors that are typical of each ego state. When a forty-year-old person changes from Adult to Child, his posture, facial expression, tone of voice, and words also change, and he becomes like his three- or four- or eight-year-old self. When he turns on his Parent ego state, we are witnessing how his real parents behaved because he literally becomes them. If you are talking to someone and feel you must help him, support him, or give him something, you are probably talking to his helpless Child. He is not really helpless, but at that moment in time he may feel, act, and see things just the way he did when he was a little child. If you are with someone and begin to feel inferior or on trial or as if you have to defend or justify yourself, you may be talking to his Critical Parent and have turned on your Not-O.K. Child.

There are four criteria which give us clues as to which ego state is dominant at the moment: (1) posture, (2) tone of voice, (3) words and phrases, and (4) situation.

When a Person is in Child

Posture: She is "all feelings," spontaneous, fetal position, wriggling, restless, eating, playing, dancing, jumping, sucking, finger in mouth or nose, cuddling, skipping, hugging, fighting, rolling on the grass or in bed, looking up (the characteristic angle at which a little kid looks at a world arranged for grownups).

Tone of Voice: She may be crying, whining, laughing, screaming, coy, angry, playful, giggly, rebellious, helpless.

Words and Phrases: She might say: "Let's play; Gimmie; Wow!; I'm great; curse words like shit, fuck; It ain't fair; Help me; I hate you; I love you; Little bitty bunny, Mommy; Gee whiz; But I can't; What should I do?; I'm so bad, weak, helpless, scared, sad; I won't; Here I go again; I never do it right; I'll do it tomorrow; I want; I'm lonely; I'm sorry; It's a big gyp; Great big lion."

Situation: She may be helpless, getting help, being fed or clothed or bathed or combed, fun, playing, creating, fighting, making love, throwing things, being judged in court or school or being bawled out by a traffic policeman or her mother or her boss, or getting her teeth drilled in a dentist's chair with a little bib under her drooling mouth.

When a Person is in Parent

NURTURING PARENT

Posture: She may be leaning forward, helping, feeding, dressing, bathing, rocking, hugging, swinging, receptive.

Tone of Voice: She is sympathetic, singing, loving.

Words and Phrases: She says things like: "Let me read you a story; There, there, sweety, I'll take care of you; Let me see where it hurts and I'll kiss it; Have some more chicken soup; Good boy! Do it again! I love you; I brought you a puppy; Come sit on Mommy's lap; Let me tuck you in."

Situation: She is helping, feeding, encouraging.

CRITICAL PARENT

Posture: She sits or stands upright, hands on hips, forefinger waving, fist clenched, military, erect.

Tone of Voice: She speaks in a voice which is loud, strong, firm, self-righteous, ordering, assured, angry, sad, fearful.

Words and Phrases: She uses lots of do's and don'ts and should's and ought's; "Be on time; Stop at a red light; Eat quietly; Don't be late, clumsy, stupid, bad, dirty; Crybaby! Come home early; Brush your teeth; Eat your cereal; This is the right way; You should, you ought, you must, be humble, bold, brave, independent, obedient; Hurry up; Don't rush; You are foolhardy; You are cowardly; Live for

18

beauty-truth-justice; Be thrifty; Don't goof off; Don't waste time; Life is hard; Don't be stingy, greedy; It would be nice if you would, but you...; Live for law and order; Honor thy father and thy mother; Are you telling the truth? You ought to finish what you start!"

Situation: She might be philosophizing, judging, criticizing, moralizing, rescuing, giving rules, supervising. The conversation might be politics, child-raising, religion, or race relations.

When a Person is in Adult

Posture: She is casual, alert, pointing out information, attending.

Tone of Voice: She speaks in a voice which is crisp, casual, clear, affectless.

Words and Phrases: She uses words which are sharp, descriptive. "It's raining now; The room is 7' x 14'; This is a hammer; I hear my stomach growling; I see you fighting; My mother is scowling and her face looks angry; I want to take your hand and I'm also aware that I'm afraid; My heart is pounding; If I stay and talk with you, I will probably miss my train."

Situation: She is perceiving, solving problems, computing, thinking, giving information, examining Child requests or Parent rules, planning work or play, counting, taking things into consideration including how people will feel, computing probabilities and weighing alternatives.

The major tasks of the Parent and Adult are to take care of the Child in a dynamically changing world, to help her figure out what she needs to satisfy that need in ways which are effective and safe. TA therapists invite each person to use her Adult and Parent in the service of her Child.

Who's in Charge Here?

We estimate that the Parent has 25% of the person's total energy and power, the Adult 30%, and the Child 45%. Some TA people think the ego states have equal power. The Adult doesn't make decisions, but it provides valuable information to the decision-making Parent or the decision-making Child. The purpose of the Adult is to take care of the Child in a changing world. The Child wants to exist and feel comfortable. The Child needs food, sleep, and exercise; she needs to be hugged and talked to and listened to. She needs excitement. The Child has different needs at different times, and the job of the Adult is to find out what the Child needs and to enable the Child to satisfy those needs in the real world without being hurt.

The Adult operates in two ways: she perceives ("I see the soup boiling over.") and she thinks. The Adult psyches out the Parent and psyches out the Child. A Gestalt therapist who asks her patient, "What do you experience *now*?" (What do you see, feel, hear, taste, smell?) is inviting the patient to turn on her Adult. In both TA and Gestalt theory, the Child (Gestalt therapists call the Child the "underdog," the Parent is the "top dog") has the most power, but if the Parent and Adult combine, they have more power than the Child. If the person feels guilty, that means the internal Parent is probably beating her Child and requiring of her Child that she feel bad. If you've got it made, your Parent and Adult are helping your Child; but if you're locked into a script whereby you're supposed to go through life frustrated, you probably accomplish this by turning your Adult off, and either don't let yourself know what you need or don't let yourself figure out how to detect your own negative reactions to people and situations or their response to you. In this way you may get stuck in a job that's lousy, marry a man who doesn't take good care of you, and set up all sorts of difficult things for yourself so that you feel rotten all of your life.

Usually people support bad feelings by thinking thoughts and stirring up unhappy memories. In this way a person who complains about feeling bad may, out of her awareness, reinforce and keep feeding her bad feelings.

Four Propositions

Here are four propositions which are important if you find that you are keeping bad feelings going by what you "think" or "remember."

1. *I can think any thoughts I wish.*
   We take for granted that I can think any thoughts I want. I can think of a pink hippopotamus with a purple tail stepping lightly on buttercups. I can think of my friend being sick. I can think of becoming Secretary of the Treasury.

2. *I can think whatever I wish about myself.*
   I can think I'm important, or not smart, or lazy, or I never do it right, or what's wrong with me, or I should have...or next time I'll....

3. *I can think whatever I wish about others.*
   I can think others will hurt me, exploit me, reject me, despise me, help me, be nice to me or ignore me.

4. *I can induce moods or feelings in myself by the thoughts I think.*
   So if I want to feel bad, I can think I'll do it wrong and then you will punish me. Or if I want to feel sad, I can remember sad times in my life; or if I want to feel angry I can think of people who hurt me; and if I want to feel scared, create some ghosts and goblins or imagine my car or plane will crash.

The Steve Karpman Drama Triangle

Now let us consider another very important stroking pattern. I'm going to talk about a drama. Here is Willy, our little hero (we're going to call him "V" for "Victim"). Its a rainy Sunday and he has nothing to do, so he goes into his big brother's room where his brother is making an airplane model. Big Brother says, "Willy, don't touch my plane. The glue is wet." Willy puts his finger on his brother's plane and the wing falls off. His brother says, "Leave it alone! You're spoiling it! Get out of my room!" Willy responds by touching the other wing. Big Brother comes over and gives him a push. Then Willy starts to cry loud enough so that his mother, who is in the kitchen, can hear. And he's got to manage the crying to make it last long enough until she gets there. As an added effect, maybe he picks yesterday's mosquito bite so he's bleeding. All set. In comes Mommy, the Rescuer. Maybe Mommy is mad to begin with because Daddy isn't home this Sunday. He's out playing golf, and she's angry at injustice everywhere. So she's ready for a passion play of Good versus Evil. And here it is! She's angry and says to Big Brother, whom we're going to call the Persecutor, "Marvin? Is something wrong with your head? You're nasty, you're mean, nobody will ever love you."

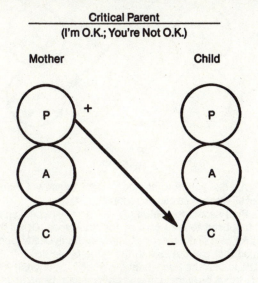

Critical Parent

(I'm O.K.; You're Not O.K.)

Mother   Child

"There's something wrong with your head."
"You're nasty and mean."
"Nobody will ever love you."

But to little Willy, she says, "You come into the kitchen with Mommy, Willy. There, there, pat, pat, have a cookie, hug, hug, hug." Marvin is getting strokes for being a bully, Willy for being hurt, and Mom for saving Good Helpless Guys from Bad Strong Guys.

Mother could say to Big Brother, "I'm sorry Willy broke your plane (C-C). I bet you feel bad that Willy broke your plane (P-C). What could you do when Willy comes in so that he doesn't break your plane? (A-A). Let's fix your plane while the glue is wet (P-C)." And Mother could say to Willy, "It's raining outside and what can you do that will be fun? (A-A). You shouldn't touch Willy's plane when he tells

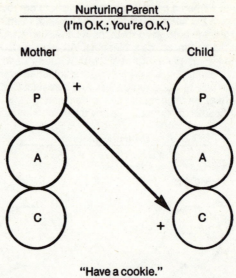

Nurturing Parent
(I'm O.K.; You're O.K.)

Mother   Child

"Have a cookie."
(hug, hug)

you not to (P-C). I like you both and don't want to see you fighting (P-C). Let's figure out what all three of us can do together (A-A)."

Sometimes the Rescuer isn't Mommy, but an older child, an older brother or sister who's supposed to take care of the little ones. Or a little child who is supposed to take care of depressed Mommy or drunk Daddy, someone like Willy who has learned that you get love in the world by getting hit first. So Willy becomes the little kid on the bus whom everybody picks on. If he and two other kids steal something, he is the one who gets caught. Later, he is the first person fired on the job. He is always in trouble. And he arranges it—that's the secret. He arranges it so he can get strokes for coming on sad sack because that's how it was when he was four. If he marries a woman who happens to be a Rescuer, who turns on to people in trouble because she got strokes for saving poor unfortunates, he can go through life with one crisis after another, and every time he's in a crisis, *she runs to take care of him*. Meanwhile, big brother Marvin, stroked for being a bad guy, is always in trouble, too. The adjustment teacher at school says he's an "acting out" child.

Once in a while, each of the people in the triangle says, "Why does this always happen to me?" But he decides he's just vulnerable. These are the words victims use: "I'm vulnerable" or "People pick on me" or "You can't trust anybody" or "I'm too trusting." Someone comes into a treatment group and says, "I don't trust anybody. People have hurt me!" There will probably be four or five Rescuers in the room who'll say, "Oh, honey! Trust us!" or "You can trust us!" And then someone else gives him a double whammy. What happens to the Rescuers? They feel bad. They've promised something they can't deliver, and after they've finished persecuting the Persecutor and begin to feel bad, they may realize that they are now also Victims and Persecutors. People who play Victim-Persecutor-Rescuer usually end up playing all three roles and feeling bad. All the players end up feeling bad. If you need to feel depressed, playing Victim-Persecutor-Rescuer will help. If you want to feel good, get some good strokes directly. Say, "I would like to talk to you. Will you talk to me?" or, "I would like a hug. Will you hug me?" You can get strokes when you feel good.

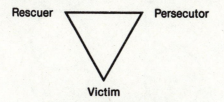

Karpman Drama Triangle

Persons in the Triangle change roles. Thus, the Rescuer becomes Persecutor and Victim; the Victim becomes Persecutor, etc.

In some families, the kids get strokes from Mommy for hassling their Daddy. Every time the kid is nasty to Daddy, Mommy gives the kid a smile. So what we often see in family therapy—and therapy with the whole family is very valuable if the therapist is skilled—is that Mommy has stroked the kid for tormenting Daddy, or Daddy has stroked the kid for bugging Mommy.

The *bragger* is a self-rescuer and people feel like shooting him down in response to his bragging. Unlike someone who has been successful and is enjoying his good fortune with child-like exuberance (to which other people usually respond with pleasure), the braggard secretly feels like a no-good flop which he covers with bragging (self-rescue). Other people respond by feeling like persecuting (completing the triangle) and showing him up. Others may not persecute the braggard, but they feel persecutory, which confirms that somewhere on the scene is a Victim and a Rescuer. In this case, the braggard is being the Victim and the Rescuer at the same time.

Contaminations

Sometimes what the patient assumes to be his Adult is really a Parent message. When two ego states overlap and blend together such that the person acts as though something he believes is really true and verifiable when it is really something his parents told him and is not true, this confusion is called Adult contaminated by Parent. Here are some examples: "Boys are bigger and smarter than girls; If you drink a quart of milk each day, you will be healthy; It's good for you if it hurts or tastes bad; Hard-to-get things are really worth having; Black people are shiftless and lazy; If it's made in the U.S.A., it's the best; Men only want one thing from girls; You get what you pay for; Pride cometh before a fall; All you need to do is love people." These statements have a ring of truth, but they are not true.

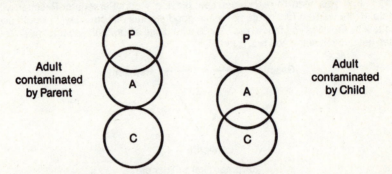

Adult
contaminated
by Parent

Adult
contaminated
by Child

The Adult may also have some weird contaminations from the Child. "They can't do without me; If I didn't show up, the club would fold; I can never make up my mind; I'm sending in 10¢ with a box top from a corn flakes box for a real submarine; I don't have to work. I can rip off groceries from the supermarts; If I walk to school a certain way or if I wear my lucky sweater, I'll get a good grade on my exam; I'm opening a new business and will make a million bucks (from someone who doesn't know how to wipe his own nose)."

The Loss of Innocence

When I was a little kid I was taught to be nice. If I let my big relatives kiss me with their wet smelly lips, finished all of my oatmeal, if I took care of my brother and sister, brushed my teeth, made in the potty, instead of in the warm bed, paid my bills, took the smallest piece of cake, kept my shirt clean, and said please and thank you, and did what my mommy wanted . . .

THEN I would be rewarded: it wouldn't rain at the picnic, my mother would like me better than my brother, my father would say he loved me, I would have my own phone, and a big desk with a view of Lake Michigan, and men and women would admire me and desire me, and when I plant a seed it would grow.

Sometime in my life I lost my innocence. I did all sorts of good things and it rained at the picnic, and my father never loved me, and I thought in dismay How could it happen to me!

Now I know that if I pay more I don't get more. I pay what I pay and I get what I get.

IV. Analyzing Transactions

The basic unit of social psychiatry is the transaction. Analyzing the transactions between two people is called transactional analysis. Transactions often involve stroking expectations. If I say, "Nice weather we are having," that means I want to talk to you. I want you to like me, to feel I'm O.K. If you answer, "Yes, beautiful weather," then we are both all right and we've stroked each other (established some pleasant contact).

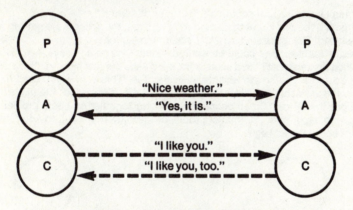

The invention of the six circles is an important symbol of communication, even as the alphabet and ten number counting system proved to be. Like the alphabet and decimals, the six circles gave us a simple way to represent complex relationships, i.e. which part of one person is talking to which part of another person.

Parallel or Complementary Transactions

A parallel transaction takes place when the addressed ego state responds. For example, Parent One says, "Kids are terrible these days," and Parent Two might respond, "Yes, they sure are." That would be a Parent-to-Parent transaction.

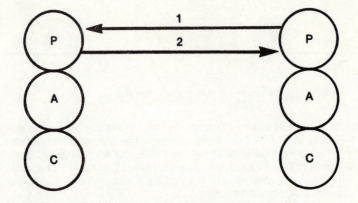

P-1: "Isn't it awful about pollution?" P-2: "Yes, it's awful."
P-1: "Isn't it too bad about the schools?" P-2: "Yes, the schools are getting worse and worse." These are *ain't it awful* parallel transactions.

Parallel transactions could be Adult-to-Adult. One person says, A-1: "How do you fix a broken radio?" In a classroom, a kid asks the teacher, A-1: "How do you spell so-and-so?" And the teacher answers, A-2: "This is how you spell it." A-1: "Pass the wrench." A-2: "Here's the wrench." A-1: "Who's got the pliers?" A-2: "I've got the pliers." When people are working together on some problem and are giving each other information, tools, or ideas, that is Adult-to-Adult, regardless of chronological age.

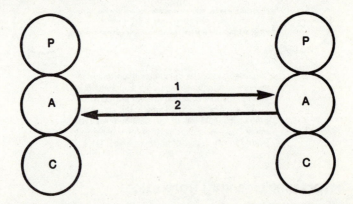

Child-to-Child transactions may be parallel. C-1: "Let's have fun!" C-2: "Yes, let's have fun." C-1: "Let's dance." C-2: "O.K., let's dance." C-1: "Let's steal hubcaps." C-2: "No, let's break windows!" All of these are Child-to-Child transactions and are parallel.

26

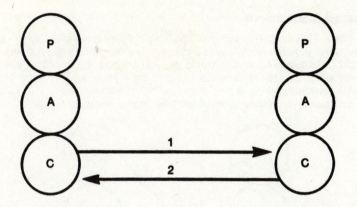

Parallel transactions can also occur between Parent and Child or Parent and Adult. The kid could say, C-1: "Mommy, I'm hungry." The Mommy would say, P-2: "O.K., here's your supper, honey."

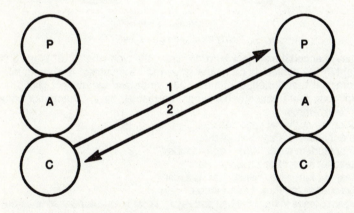

Or the husband could say to the wife, C-1: "I feel bad." And the wife might say, P-2: "Lie down, sweety, here's a hot water bottle for you," or P-2: "Why don't you take your pills?" or P-2: "You should rest." These are Child-to-Parent transactions followed by Parent-to-Child transactions. Berne said THE FIRST LAW OF COMMUNICATION IS THAT PARALLEL TRANSACTIONS CAN CONTINUE INDEFINITELY.

Crossed Transactions

A crossed transaction is different. The husband says to his wife, "Where is the typewriter?" (Adult-to-Adult—he is presumably seeking information). If she were responding Adult-to-Adult, she would say, "The typewriter is in the front hall closet," or "It is in the repair shop. I took it there yesterday." That would be a parallel transaction (A-A). But, if she says, "Why don't you ever put it away? If you put it away, you'd know where it is!" she turns on her Parent (P-C).

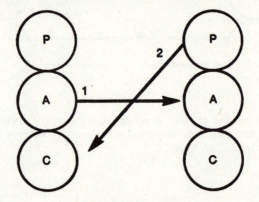

1. "Where is it?"
2. "Why don't you put it away?"

She has changed the subject from "Where is the typewriter?" to "Why don't you do right?" The subject is no longer *typewriter*, the subject is *You are not O.K.* In a crossed transaction, communication stops and the subject changes. In a schoolroom, this frequently happens: The teacher says, "Open your books to page twenty-three."
A student says: "What page, teacher?"
The teacher says: "Page twenty-three."
Another student says: "What page, teacher?"
The teacher says: "Page twenty-three."
Another student says: "What page, teacher?"
The teacher says: "Page twenty-three."
A student comes in from the hall and says: "What are we supposed to be doing?"
The teacher says: "Open your book to page twenty-three."

This is all Adult, you see, giving and getting information in a casual, alert tone of voice. But when the teacher says, "Where are your ears?" or "How many times do I have to tell you?" she is changing her ego state from her Adult to her Parent. She is changing the subject from *page twenty-three* to *something is wrong with you.* This, THE SECOND LAW OF COMMUNICATION IS THAT IN A CROSSED TRANSACTION, COMMUNICATION STOPS OR THE SUBJECT CHANGES.

28

Duplex, Angular and Ulterior Transactions

Some tricky transactions appear to be directed toward one ego state, but are actually aimed at another. One person appears to be talking to the Adult of the other person, but is actually talking to the Child (or to the Parent) of the other. The preceding illustration in which the husband asks his wife, "Where is the typewriter?" could be straight information-seeking, in which case, it would be diagrammed as follows:

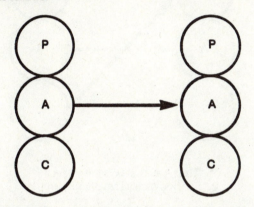

Or it could be the opening statement in an ulterior transaction which brings the secret message to her Child, "I expect you to keep track of our belongings," in which case the transaction would be diagrammed as follows:

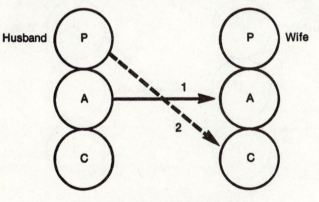

1. "Where is the typewriter?"
2. "I expect you to keep track of our belongings."

And when she answers, "The typewriter is in the hall closet," she is also saying, "I agree it is my job to keep track of our belongings. See how nicely I am doing that!"

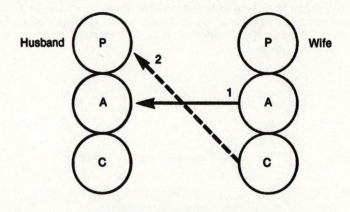

1. "The typewriter is in the closet."
2. "See how nicely I am doing that!"

Or it could be the opening shot of a game, because the husband knows that if he asks, she will get angry; and if she gets angry, he won't have to buy her a birthday present, or he will have an excuse to get drunk or have an affair.

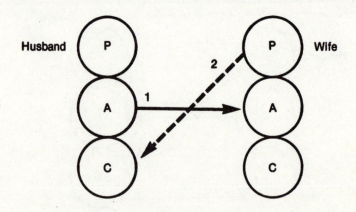

1. "Where is the typewriter?"
2. "Why don't you put things away? You never help around the house!"

A man meets a woman he's attracted to at an art museum and, over coffee, in the museum cafeteria, he asks, "Do you like etchings?" which sounds like a question to her Adult, but is actually an invitation to her Child.

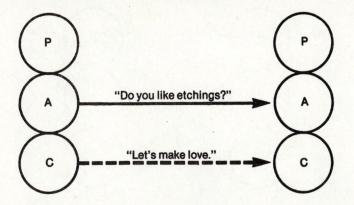

And when she says she loves etchings, she is giving more than Adult information about her artistic interests. Her Child is giving consent.

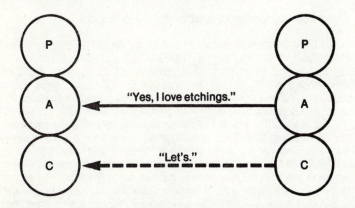

Lots of sales pitches are of this variety, masking seduction of the Child with what looks like Adult information. "Go your own way. Smoke X cigarettes." The hook is really to the Child ("You can be an independent HE MAN if you smoke X cigarettes.").

Ostensibly, directed toward the consumer's Adult: "Nobody can tell you to use this hair dye, except your mother." The picture shows a lady fondling her son. The message to her Child is, "You can use hair dye and still be a good, conventional woman, not a hussy." There is an even more subtle message to her Child which is: "Use this hair dye and you will live the American Dream, *i.e.,* a house, a husband, and 2½ children to love you."

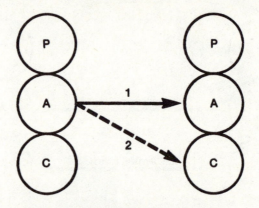

1. "Nobody can tell you to use hair dye."
2. "If you use Molly's hair freshener, you will have a nice house, a husband and children to love you."

The Third Law of Communication and Contracts

A THIRD LAW OF COMMUNICATION IS THAT WHEN THERE ARE DUPLEX TRANSACTIONS, THAT IS, WHEN THINGS ARE GOING ON AT TWO EGO LEVELS, THE MORE PRIMITIVE (CHILD) TRANSACTIONS WILL DETERMINE WHAT HAPPENS NEXT. This is so because the Child ego state has more power and energy at his or her disposal. The Parent ego state has about 25% of the power, the Adult has 30%, and all the rest of the power, 45%, is in the Child. Thus, if there is a conflict within the person between what the Parent wants and what the Child wants, the Child wins. Typically, one finds a person saying, "I should be studying for my exam tomorrow (Parent) and I want to go to the movies (Child)." In that kind of conflict, either she will go to the movies or she will stay home, but not study, even if the book is open. The Child ego state wins. A patient in therapy might say, "I want to lose weight." Lots of people lose weight. But they have a Parent rule which says, "If you lose something, you should go find it." So a contract to lose weight leaves much to be desired. The therapist might say, "What's that about?" The patient might say, "I should look my best at all times." If it's my patient, I think, "If that's the reason you want to lose weight, we might as well forget it because your Parent wants you to look your best, but your Child does not, and the Parent won't win." In other words, the treatment contract with the patient is more likely to be carried out if it is made with the approval of all three ego states. If she says, "I'm afraid I'll die, and

I want to live. I want to live and have fun," that sounds like her Child. But if she says, "One must be healthy," or "One must look his best," or "My husband wants me to," that sounds like her Parent or Adapted Child, and she's not going to lose weight. So in treatment, we want to make a contract with all three ego states to have a successful outcome. If the patient says, "I want to stop drinking because I'm scared I'll get sick," then that could be the Child. "I'm scared" is Child talk. If she says, "I can't hold a job if I drink so much," maybe her Child doesn't want to hold a job. In treatment or problem-solving groups, the big trip is to find out what a person wants and how she can get her Adult working so as to get what she wants in a safe way.

Fred's Child says, "Hey, look! I want to do that!" His Adult says, "It's possible," and his Parent says, "Good boy! You can do lots of good things." One or two percent of the population have this going for them; they are the creative people. They have all kinds of permissions. The Parent says, "You got an idea, kid? It's probably a real good idea, so go ahead and do it." That's different from the Parent who frequently says, "Stop. You're going to get into trouble." That kind of Parent doesn't say, "Good boy, go ahead and do it." That Parent predicts, "Everything you do, you mess up. You're going to ruin your life. You're going to end up in jail." Kids believe their parents and make it happen the way their parents predict. This is called a self-fulfilling prophecy ("I always knew I would end up behind bars."). Here is a baby boy, a few weeks old, lying there, naked. His mother had taken off his diaper and he has touched his erect penis in his squirming around. Mommy said, "Damn!! The kid is a sex maniac!" She could just as well say, "Good boy, you can do it." She's afraid that many perfectly normal acts are crazy, and teaches her baby to be afraid and ashamed of his normal instincts.

In his book, *Sex In Human Loving,* Berne names three kinds of people: winners, losers, and almost winners. And we might add another kind—"almost losers." A person with a tragic script starts taking a lot of risks, stepping out in front of cars, not fastening his seat belt, going for bigger stakes. He is tied into the excitement of the Almost. And when the situation changes, he arranges another so that his Child is into the excitement again of Almost. He is hooked into excitement, and can have excitement skiing or speeding without safety belts buckled or robbing gas stations, or chasing women.

This third law of communication is very important then when making contracts because the person's Child, the most powerful part of him, may be running the show for better or for worse, saving the person, or doing him in, putting the person's power and skill in support of the contract or in opposition to it.

Relationships (Staying Together)

In most full, rich relationships, parent with child, husband with wife, there are many ties holding the parties together—or many reasons for them to stay together. Some relationships seem rich and rewarding, while others indicate that certain ways of being together are avoided. With a married couple, there may be some kid-to-kid stuff going on (C-C). They go out and have fun, roll in the leaves, have a snowball fight, enjoy sex, tell one another secrets, kid-to-kid, like, she might say, "You're a dirty rat" (instead of saying, "You're hostile," which implies she is O.K. and he is not O.K.). If she says, "You're a rat," and he says, "You're a slob," then it's kid-to-kid fight, and nobody's "holier than thou."

In most relationships that are viable, that is, likely to continue, the A-A line of communication also is open. The two are solving problems. He says, "Gee, the Ford's got X this year, but the Chevy offers XYZ." She says, "Model Z is most apt to start in cold weather."

With most couples who have a viable relationship, there's some Parent-to-Parent activity also going on. She may say, "The President is a liar. He's just getting us deeper and deeper into war." And he might say, "Yes, look where our taxes are going." Or he might say, "The radicals these days want to wreck everything," and she says, "It's disgusting! I don't know where Americanism has gone." The P-P line of communication is open. "Isn't it terrible about kids?" "We should give so-and-so a present. Her husband got sick. We should go see him in the hospital."

In an open relationship, a woman's Child has something going with his Parent. She says, "Gee, the clutch on my car doesn't work. What should I do?" and he says, "Did you try XYZ?" or "I'll have a look at it." And sometimes the reverse is going on, i.e., transactions between his little boy and her mommy. He'll say, "The button's off my shirt," and she'll say, "I'll fix it." Or he'll say, "God, I think I'm getting a cold," and she'll say, "You've been working too hard, I'll run you a hot bath." So you can see all the lines of communication holding people together. With all that going, if one or another line is closed, there are still several lines open. There are still lots of ways they can transact (i.e., stroke one another). If her little girl gets mad at him and doesn't talk to him or sleep with him or fight with him, there is still putting bookcases together and moralizing together and fixing the clutch. She is still taking care of his cold, and he is still fixing her car. The relationship has enough ties to exist. They are stroking each other in lots of different ways. If all they have going is big-daddy-to-little-girl transactions, like the chorus girl and the businessman (Big-Daddy-to-Bunny-Boo), that's pretty limiting to both of them. Furthermore, they probably won't last together because when they get angry and her little girl feels put down by his Parent and she stops investing energy in stroking his Parent, there are no bonds keeping them together, no other avenues for stroking one another.

If this is a woman who can only function in the Child ego state, and then she has a son or daughter, she's in trouble. She calls her mother on the telephone and says, "I don't know what to do with this baby!" She has turned off her Parent and Adult. Everybody has a Parent, Adult and Child; but some people don't turn on their Parent or their Adult, or some people don't turn on their Child. So, if the woman has a baby and she won't turn on her Parent to the baby, she may feel like this: "Well, when the baby's born, the baby will take care of me." Many mothers and fathers feel that way. And when the baby cries, mother feels criticized, like the baby is saying, "You're not a good Mommy," and she may even attack the baby and severely injure it.

34

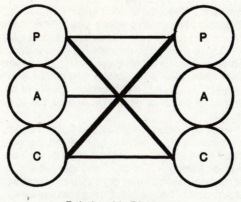

Relationship Diagram

In a strong relationship, there are many lines of
communication open holding the two people together.

Symbiotic Relationships

At birth, the child has no Parent or Adult ego state. He or she is all Child ("I want what I want when I want it, or I'll scream until I get what I want."). The mother may turn off her own Child ego state so that she is willing to wake up at 2:00 a.m. to feed her baby and do lots of things her Child may not feel like doing, like

Mother   Child

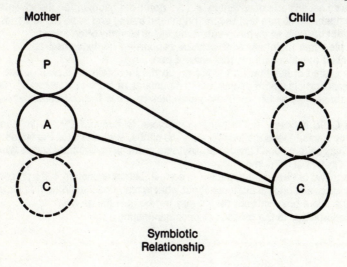

**Symbiotic
Relationship**

35

getting out of a warm bed. Sometimes we see this in a husband-wife relationship where the husband is Parent and Adult and the wife is Child or vice versa, or in a parent-adolescent relationship where one is Parent and Adult and the other is Child. Jacqui and Aaron Schiff stimulated a great deal of interest and thinking among T.A. therapists, about symbiosis. Books and research reports have been written on symbiosis by Margaret Mahler and others in the psychoanalytic community since 1949. A symbiotic relationship is one in which two people together appear to make one whole person. One does all the work, while the other stays in bed or drinks or carries on or feels too scared or sick to do anything.

One is allowed to work, take care of, criticize, and figure things out, and the other is allowed to be taken care of, be criticized, get saved, pampered, or punished. If his agreement was to be Big Daddy, and hers to be Bunny Boo, then if he says, "I want to have fun, go fishing or play golf," she may get very angry because he is violating the agreement, and she may get sicker or scared which induces him to stay home and take care of her (*i.e.*, keep things as they were).

Analyzing symbiotic relationships gets pretty tricky because it becomes hard to tell who is taking care of whom, *i.e.*, does one party get sick or helpless to support the wellness and power of the other, or vice versa? Probably both, and lots of illness and craziness and bad feelings arise out of one person in a symbiosis adapting himself to the needs of the other by becoming helpless or helpful, overactive or passive, smart or stupid—to support the other. Berne (*Games People Play*, 1964, p. 105) says, ". . . a woman marries a domineering man so that he will restrict her activities and keep her from getting into situations that frighten her. If this were a simple operation, she might express her gratitude. . . In the game If It Weren't For You, however, her reaction is quite the opposite: she. . .complains about the restrictions which makes her spouse feel uneasy and gives her all sorts of advantages. . . ." Berne did not mention the advantages to the husband: he can feel secure, bright and strong and avoid his fear that she might not be there when he comes home, as his Mommy often wasn't.

People often maintain symbiosis by supporting contaminated adults (lies). They need to believe things that are not true.

"I'm scared of heights. So I won't go up the mountain (or elevator). See this newspaper article (about people lost in mountains or stuck in elevators)." People maintain strange beliefs by finding examples to prove their contaminations are true.

The Child believes "If I'm hungry, everyone is hungry." Or "If I'm hungry, mommy wants to feed me." Or "If I like the circus, everyone likes the circus. The Child may believe I don't have to do anything because my mommy knows what to do. If I'm lost she'll come find me.

At age two or three contamination is normal. Decontamination is the process of growing up, and finding out more about what is real, understanding that people's feelings about how we want things may not be how things are.

Psychotherapy is the process of decontaminating.

V. Structuring Time

People are born and then they die. What they do in between we call "structuring time." The problem is what will I do with my life? Some of the ways people structure time bring lots of strokes; others bring few strokes. The six ways to structure time in increasing order of risk and stroke potentials are:

1. Withdrawing
2. Rituals
3. Procedures
4. Pastimes
5. Games
6. Intimacy

People learn to structure time when they are children. Mommy says, in effect, "Honey, this is the way to live."

Withdrawing

Withdrawing is the least risky and least strokey way to spend time. Sleeping, daydreaming, counting your blessings or your faults are examples. Some people seem to be here and listening, but they have actually withdrawn their attention. They have left the Now. A woman may talk about her husband, who is not present, or about what she felt yesterday or about what might happen tomorrow. Everyone has a closed circuit television set in his or her head, where old movies may be played from the marvelous collection of memories of the past. We all have very effective ways to tune out what is going on around us and, instead, attend to the memories or fantasies in our heads. Some people are never where they are. When they are brushing their teeth, they are thinking about working; when eating, they think about their date; when with their date, they think about the dentist. What kind of strokes do we get from withdrawal? The answer is any kind we want. With the help of fantasy or memory, we can induce almost any mood. Everyone has had experiences about which he feels very sad. Want to be sad? Remember those sad times or even imagine some that might happen. Everyone has had experiences in which she felt unjustly treated. Want to feel angry? Tune out what is going on around you and tune in "remember when so-and-so did me in." People learn to withdraw by watching parents who withdraw, also by getting strokes for sitting passively and not making waves while things are going on in the here and now that are boring, unpleasant, or undesirable. Years later, Mommy in my head says, "You're a good kid. You're polite. You don't make trouble or say unpleasant things or complain. Everyone will like you. Sit through this boring lecture, honey, tune it out, smile, and look interested and I will love you." I sit there for a while and think,

"See what a nice person I am!" Although some amount of withdrawal is essential (all people must sleep), some people are withdrawn a great portion of their lives. We say they are usually in their heads rather than living in the Now.

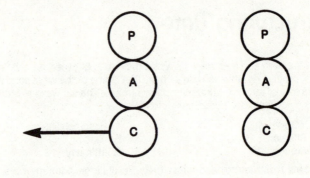

Withdrawal

Rituals

Another way people structure time is with rituals. Rituals are Parent-programmed. That means there is a strong element of "This is what you should do" in rituals. When you go to a funeral, there are ways to look and dress and things to say that'are proper and some that are improper. The same is true of a wedding. There are "should's" and "ought's" about many rites of passage: what to do when a baby is born, what to do when someone dies. Some people ritualize all of their lives: this is what you have for breakfast; that's Daddy's chair; dinner is at 6:00 p.m.; what you eat for dinner must be different from what you eat for breakfast; you have sex Tuesday, Thursday, and Saturday at 11:00 p.m., and you start by doing thus and so. Everything is programmed and ordered, no surprises, no risks. That's one of the beauties of rituals; they are predictable. No scary stuff, even about pleasure. For example, you're asked to somebody's house for dinner. You probably can guess the exact time you're going to eat, roughly what you're going to eat, what they'll give you to drink, the kind of furniture you're going to sit on, what the conversation's going to be about, what people will wear, and when you're going to go home. It's possible to ritualize the living room, bathroom, bedroom, dining room, Christmas, dating, sex, work, and conversation. There are also stroking rituals. The newspaper boy says, "Hello, Mr. Cursey," and you respond, "Hi, nice day" (two strokes). You may have a two-stroke ritual with the newsboy and an eight-stroke ritual with a neighbor. You may have a sixteen-stroke ritual with the fellow who works at the next desk. If you have a two-stroke ritual set up and you give someone sixteen strokes, he may say to himself, "Hmmm, I wonder what's wrong with Charley? He usually gives me a quick 'hello' but today he went on and on!" When you ask, "How are you?" some people are supposed to say, "Fine," no matter how they feel. If we tell them how we are, they may think, "What a pain in the neck that guy is. What a hypochondriac. Doesn't he know I'm supposed to ask how he is and he's supposed to say, 'fine'?" The question is not really to gather information. It is to stroke. And you are supposed to answer correctly. When you say, "Nice weather," the other person is expected to say, "Yes, beautiful," which means I like you and we can talk. If you say, "Nice weather," and he replies, "Lousy weather," then watch out. That's probably a duplex transaction with the other person's Child saying, "Let's fight." This is no longer a ritual, but we are moving into the more exciting stuff of which games are made.

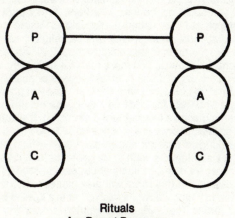

**Rituals
Are Parent Programs**

Procedures

Procedures are Adult-programmed. That means they are a series of transactions using one's Adult to solve some problem or make something. To get a particular job, the procedure might be to fill out an application. The application directs us to "print" not write. The seeker after truth, beauty, justice or health and wealth uses procedures, but may also be withdrawing from family and friends. Some people learn from early life that they are supposed to "make stuff" or "take lessons," in their "free" time. They get taken to ballet school and piano lessons. They study how to recognize birds and tie knots and water-ski and paste stamps in a book. At a party, the hostess might prefer to go into the kitchen and make the salad rather than come out and be with everybody. She's a Girl Scout all grown up. She's supposed to be making things to get strokes. Just being isn't enough. Hobby people are deeply involved in procedures. The surgeon uses procedures to take out tonsils; the mechanic uses procedures to fix a car; the lawyer uses procedures to get a client out of jail. Procedures are a little more unpredictable than rituals and therefore a little more risky. The issue with a procedure is not whether it is "proper" but rather, if it works. Someone may come up and talk to you while you are making a salad, and if procedures offer more unprogrammed opportunities for kicks and kisses than did withdrawing and rituals, you may come up with some never-before-tried innovative method for making the salad. All of which introduces more Child excitement and variety.

Pastimes

Pastimes are parallel transactions. General Motors: How do you like your Ford? Let me tell you about my Pontiac. Wardrobe: Pretty print on your blouse. Do you like the long skirts? PTA: school, kids; recipes. Pastimes can be P-P (Isn't it awful about...husbands, politics, race, prices, religion, schools?); they can be A-A (Is there a TV repairman in this neighborhood? Which hotel in Bermuda? Know a good mechanic? How do you mix a real Martini?); they can be C-C (Let's get Charlie. Let's dance or get drunk or steal hubcaps or pull Miriam's new wig); they can be C-P (What do I do with a wife like that? Can you give me some advice about a six-year-old who wets the bed? I'd like to lose ten pounds...on my last diet I...Where can a divorcee like me find a man?...). It's important to understand that pastimes (diet, depression, alcoholism, wife) are used instead of thinking, instead of working to change; and in pastimes—which are parallel transactions—the kid is watching and waiting for game players. If I'm waiting to play "rapo" with someone, we may be talking about cars or food or fashion, but I'm really looking to see who in this room will play games with me. So while we're into this boring stuff in which we stroke each other in a low-keyed way, I'm psyching out players for games. That's where the exciting strokes are.

Games

A game is a series of transactions which structure time, provide strokes, further the life script, confirm the life position, and give a payoff; it follows a predictable path and often ends up with bad feelings for all players. Eric Berne wrote an entire book describing many different games and how people play them.* Games may also be analyzed in other ways, among them:

Con ⟶ Gimmick ⟶ Response ⟶ X Switch ⟶ Payoff

or

1 ⟶ 2 ⟶ 3 ⟶ 4 ⟶ 5

* *Games People Play* (New York: Grove Press, 1962).

or

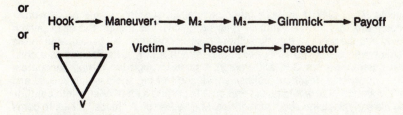

or

All of these describe qualities Berne talks about in his book. Frank Ernst, Jr. reports that at any point after the first move the player may return to a previous position or go on to the next one. Thus, his moves may be coded 1, 2, 3, 2, 3, 4, 5, 2, 3, 1, 4, 5, 1, 2, 1, and so on, with each number representing his own unique steps.** Thus, an "I'll get sick to get your attention—please-don't-leave-me" player may go through the following moves:

1. I'm not sure what to work on. (It's not important). I have this funny feeling in my head.
2. Now it's moved to my chest. (I've got your attention).
3. I'm beginning to feel better. (Other player looks away or moves two inches backward).
4. Oh, it's back again. Terrible. I'm so confused, poor me. You must help me. Why are you leaving me? (Player moves five inches away). I'm getting angry! All I wanted was a little help so I could pull myself together.
5. I hate you! (Cries) I'm so bad! And runs out of the room.

Often, people who have learned that suffering is the best way to get "mommy" strokes get some and begin to feel better, but then renew the old pain when mommy withdraws and repeat the whole process of suffering ⟶ rescue ⟶ improvement ⟶ relapse.

This is Frank Ernst, Jr.'s idea about how people may play a particular part of a game over and over again, maybe never playing it out to the end. That is frequently observed in the game of "Dry Alchoholic," or "Food Addict," in which a person wants to interest all the mommies present in her unhappiness about being overweight, and our heroine convinces the mommies present that she really wants to lose weight this time. Often this is accompanied by an eager request for diet information (actually, most obese people know more about diets than non-obese people, so the request is some kind of pretended ignorance, i.e., con.)

Our heroine reports weight loss through several subsequent sessions, which delights all the helpful mommies present and leads them to believe that our heroine is on the right track, has solved the problem, and the helpful mommies can start to look for other troubled people to help. Then, one week our heroine reports she is starting to gain weight again. Everyone who gets involved in a game has some stake in keeping it going. People don't play games *against* other

**Franklin Ernst, Jr., *The Game Diagram,* Vallejo, CA, Addresso'Set, 1972.

people. They play them *with* other people. Frequently, people accuse other people they are involved with of "playing games," as though the other person could engage them in a game without their cooperation. All participants in the game have an ax to grind. For example, Person A may have decided as a child that parents are not O.K. and Person A goes through life having encounters with supervisors, teachers, policemen, all sorts of big shots which usually end on a sour note. We would guess Person A is putting a lot of energy into confirming his early decision about authorities. Maybe Person A "helps" things to come out sour. One day, Person A meets Doctor B. Doctor B decided at an early age that the world was an unjust place, and that no matter how hard he tried he would get it in the neck. When Person A and Doctor B play games, these will be a series of transactions which will enable each of them to confirm the early decision with which each came to the encounter. Perhaps Person A will ask Doctor B for something which both Person A's and Doctor B's Parents believe he "ought" to give (money, telephone time in the wee hours of the morning, credit, sympathy, etc.). Then when Doctor B may find he is overextending himself and he says he does not wish to give Person A any more extra goodies, Person A can say, "See, I always knew it. You guys are all alike. Just in it for what you can get." And Doctor B's Child can say again, "It ain't fair. The least Person A could do is to appreciate what I've already given. Why does this always happen to me? I try so hard to be a good guy and I end up kicked."

Games start with a quiet, sneaky warm prickly combined with a very visible warm fuzzy. When the game begins, players turn their Adults off and continue in Child ego states, that is, they just see the warm part. Games look like, "Come here, and we'll feel good together." A very common game is "Why Don't You? . . . Yes, But . . ." (WDYYB). X says, "I have this problem," and Y says, "O.K., I have the answer," and if X says, "Thank you," there's no game. But if X keeps getting answers but feels they are not the right answers (instead of a parallel transaction, A-A, there is a secret message from X's Child to your Parent, saying, "You'll never satisfy me"), X does not really want information or advice. He wants strokes and a fight with your Parent. So the dramatic shift in a game occurs when someone shifts from helpless Child or inviting Child into critical Parent who clobbers the other Child. Or someone shifts into critical Child who clobbers the other "trying-to-help" Parent for doing it wrong or not really helping ("You promised to make me happy and see, I'm still not happy.").

Some games can only be played with two people, but with "Yes, but" up to a thousand can play. A new school superintendent can say, "How do I get good principals?" to a group of old superintendents and they can give him solutions from now until doomsday, and he'll always win because he can say, "Yes, but I have already tried those." The purpose of this game may be to prove that the Parents (old-timers, big shots, bosses, people in authority) are not O.K.

Or, the purpose may be to confirm an early "life is going to be one frustration after another." Perhaps when he was having fun as a child, a grown-up came in and said, "Yes it would be nice to do that, but we can't do everything we like. You can't do that!" Later on, every time he has a nice fantasy, he interrupts it. He has learned to turn on a frustrating Parent to deprive his yearning Child. A male yes-butter may frustrate himself by dreaming of being with his girlfriend and in the dream, just as she undresses, her father walks in.

Or he wants to go into business for himself "yes, but" he "but's" himself out of it. Everything after the "but" erases everything before the "but." "I'd love to go on a vacation, but all my work would pile up and be waiting for me when I got home" means "I'm not going."

In a two-handed game, one player may feel self-righteous and the other feels not O.K. and bad, and both get a lot of good and bad strokes. The good guy also gets Parent strokes in his head from Mom or Dad who told him never to trust people in the first place; and the bad guy gets strokes in his head from Mom or Dad who predicted he would screw up and always mess things up and never do anything right.

If you have decided at age twelve or thirteen that you might commit suicide, then you play games that move you toward that end (kick me, harried, and the like). You'll manage to get it in the neck at the end of each game. You may have it in your head that when you get 38,000 kicks, that's when you get to go, guilt-free. Anyone who has suffered so much has a right to knock himself off.

Games are the way each of the participants works out her own, private, individual structural conflicts with other people. We use the word structural to refer to what is going on within a person, what is going on between the Adult, Parent, and Child of one person. Transactional analysis is what goes on between two or more persons. Suppose I have a battle going on inside of me: my Child likes sex but my Parent says, "No, that's bad." I have a structural conflict. So what do I do when I meet someone else with a similar conflict? We play a rapo game, each of us getting the other guy involved in our structural conflicts. We start by giving one another Child "Let's" messages. Then, just before we have sex, one of us turns on a moralistic disapproving Parent that is like the other's, and the one who turns on the "disapprover" kicks the other one. That way, we both avoid sex, and one of us takes the "bad guy" rap for both of us having appeared the more willing.

Usually, somebody gets kicked in a game, for the reason that most people who are playing games feel something is wrong, and they choose up for who is going to catch it. If two people have the same kind of structural conflict and find each other, they have a subtle agreement that one of them will take the guilt, and the other is going to dish it out. If you are catching it in the neck all the time, you probably made some script decision early in your life about being victimized or about suffering. Dibs on the one who gets kicked! For instance, I'm supposed to get kicked, and you pick that up from my "poor little me," "excuse me," "helpless" gestures. If you are supposed to do the kicking, we are a pair made in heaven. If, however, you are supposed to get kicked too, you leave me quickly and find somebody else who is supposed to do the kicking, and you probably find that other person more exciting and "attractive" than you do me. When the therapist sees a game in his group, the therapist has four alternatives: (1) play the game; (2) ignore it; (3) identify it; or (4) change it.

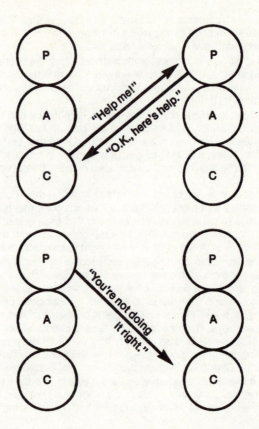

Intimacy

Intimacy is a risky way of structuring time, and may be the most rewarding. It's a Child-to-Child transaction with openness, awareness, and spontaneity, and it's usually in the Now. You let whomever you're being intimate with know what you are feeling Now. This is based on trust. Lots of people confuse sex with intimacy. Sex can be a way of withdrawing, can be a ritual, procedure, pastime or game, as well as a way of being intimate.

Some people are capable of a number of intimate relationships, and others go through their lives without one. Intimacy is when a person says something about himself. "I have a headache," "I like you," "I'm bored," or "I'm mad at you," pitched from one person's Child to the other person's Child may be an invitation for intimacy. (The same phrase pitched from my Child to your Parent is more likely to be an invitation to a game.)

Intimacy need not be verbal, as when a mother holds her infant and they look at each other lovingly.

Did you ever see two kids splashing in the mud in their new shoes, and both giggling at each other? That's intimacy (with a little *kick me* in the near future). Or lovers gazing into each other's eyes. Or two kids who have a plan to torment their teacher. There is a look which expresses "we're together and in touch with one another," which is intimate and personal.

In some families, people are taught not to be intimate. You see a man with a humpback and you hear a kid ask in a very loud voice, "Mommy, what's wrong with that man's back?" If Mommy acts as though no one is supposed to acknowledge what's going on, that the man doesn't know something is wrong with his back and that other people also can see that something is wrong with his back and says, "Shhh! Don't say anything!" then the child could be learning, "Don't say what you're thinking or feeling. Don't be open, don't be curious, don't let others know where you're at in your head. If you're open and intimate, people can't take it." Some don't-be-intimate messages take the form, "Don't talk to people, people will hurt you" or "You are not O.K., and if you get close to people, you will hurt them" or "Don't bother me with your feelings, I can barely handle my own" or "Who needs you?" or "If you can't say something nice, don't say anything."

What's Important?*

Therapist: Tell your daughter what you want of her.

Father: I want you to get married and have children.

Therapist to daughter: How do you reply?

Daughter: He tells me what he wants. He doesn't ask me. He wants to be famous and be remembered.

Father: What is important to you?

Daughter: What is important to me is to be loved by the Person who I love. To love someone and be loved.

*Thanks to Myrna S. Haimowitz for this.

VI. Life Positions

There are four life positions, and each person holds one of the four and sees things in a particular manner that goes with that position. For example, a person can have the life position that I'm O.K. and you're O.K., or, I'm O.K. and you're not O.K., or I'm not O.K. and you're O.K., or we're both not O.K. There is a difference of opinion among TA therapists as to what position the child holds at birth. According to Thomas Harris, the child is born not O.K. because she is helpless at birth and must depend on others to keep her alive. Berne's theory is that every infant is born a princess or prince; she's O.K., unless she has bad experiences and decides to be a frog. Then somewhere along the way, the child decides that she's O.K. or she's not O.K., and she decides if other people are O.K. or not O.K.

Harris says the little child can't do much without his parents, so he gets into a position that he's really not O.K., and he can't function without them. Suppose a child is O.K. but is having a rough time because his parents are sick or the mother's scared because the father's unemployed and alcoholic, so she gives the baby "Who-needs-you? You-are-a-burden-and-not-O.K." messages. The child decides "I'm not O.K." If somewhere along the line, such a child comes into treatment, maybe when he's eight or fifteen or forty-five, and a therapist or facilitator might say to him, "You have this position that you're not O.K. That's a decision you made when you were two or five years old, and you're putting lots of energy and care into keeping it going. Let's turn your Adult onto the question of how you keep it going." The person made the decision in the first place and can change it anywhere along the line.

The decision that a person is O.K. is extremely helpful when a person has troubles. The O.K. decision is: I've got problems and I can do something about them. An example of the frog position is: I'm not O.K., so I have to play helpless or angry or confused or sad or scared or deprived to get strokes from you super O.K. people. Other frogs live in a you're not O.K. life. If the three-year-old in the family makes all the decisions about the house because his mother is drunk or depressed or "insecure," he gets the feeling that he's O.K. and the other people around him are not O.K. He may firm up an "I'm not O.K., you're O.K." position. Everyone is bad. People are helpless but they will not get the help they need. He may ask help from somebody he intuitively knows can't or won't help him, thereby acting like a jerk and proving that neither of them is O.K. Berne talked about the "prick," the "sulk," and the "jerk." The jerk is not helping people; he only tries to help. Offering to serve the coffee, he spills it and then accidentally breaks the dish and says I'm sorry, and he feels sad.

THE OK CORRAL
(Dr. Franklin H. Ernst, Jr.)

You're OK

I'm Not OK You're OK – + *Get Away From*	I'm OK You're OK + + *Get On With*
I'm Not OK You're Not OK – – *Get Nowhere*	I'm OK You're Not OK + – *Get rid of*

I'm OK

For children and adults not familiar with corrals, Dr. S. Otho Hesterly in *How To Use Transactional Analysis in the Public Schools,* Little Rock, 1974, has revised this concept to the OK House. People mark the room they are in, and when they feel differently, they go to the OK House on the wall and show how they have moved from one room to another.

THE OK HOUSE
(Dr. S. Otho Hesterly)

You're OK

The I'm Not OK You're OK Room *Helpless*	The I'm OK You're OK Room *Happy*
The I'm Not OK You're Not OK Room *Hopeless*	The I'm OK You're Not OK Room *Angry*

I'm OK

VII. Feelings

There are at least three kinds of feeling experiences. The first one is called a *reaction,* the second is a *racket,* and the third is a *rubberband.* They all feel real, and it is not always easy to tell from the feeling end whether one is reacting, engaging in a racket, or rubberbanding. However, transactional analysts respond very differently to reactions than they do to rackets and rubberbands, and we believe it is important to decide which of these is occurring.

Reactions

A reaction or reactive feeling is the person's feeling in response to something that's happening right now. Reaction = FN (feeling now). For example, if I trip over something as I walk down the street, I may hurt my toe. I might say, "Ouch! Damn it!" That is a reaction. I got divorced yesterday and cried all day. That's a natural reaction after a twenty-year marriage. Or if a dear one dies, we expect someone to feel sad for a while. Many religions permit a year of mourning. But a year from now, it's over. Not thirty years of sadness over the loss of some family member. Frank has a very sad, almost crying quality in his voice. We find that Frank did not mourn at his father's funeral. If I don't cry, he's not really dead, and I'll think he is alive, so instead of mourning and having the mourning done with, Frank didn't mourn openly but grieves quietly for many years. Or, Susan wins a tennis match, so she feels good. Reactive feelings are changing all the time. A person who is in touch with her feelings will know when she is hungry or tired or curious or wanting strokes. Awareness of your own feelings helps you to get what you want. If Sally has a reaction to some event, we encourage her to feel it rather than help her avoid reactive-sad or reactive-mad feelings. If she was not permitted to feel her sadness or anger as a child, we help her to reexperience the old event, feel the original forbidden feeling, and be done with it, to thereby finish the old unfinished business.

After a year or two, most infants stop reacting spontaneously. They have learned to show feelings which are stroked and to stop feelings from which parents withdraw or to which they respond "coolly." Thus, little Willy, aged 4, goes to the dentist. Mom says, "Be brave." That means, "Let the dentist hurt you and don't let him know. Don't show your pain." Let people hurt you and if you let anyone know you are not brave, you are not O.K. How incredibly cruel. And counter to all the energy Mom is putting into providing for, helping and protecting Willy; also it contrasts with all the "take care of yourself" messages.

Rackets and the Human Body

Racket Definition

A racket is an old feeling not reactive to the current situation, based on a long-range system of beliefs, supported and confirmed by selective perceptions, and accompanied by muscular, chemical-electrical changes in the body.

Initially transactional, a racket is learned and reinforced by stroking, usually by the parents or other caretakers. Later, when the caretaker is internalized, the person provides his own strokes, and the reinforcement becomes internal and structural. Other people may also stroke, reinforce or support a racket, but the major source of reinforcement comes from the Parent.

A racket has several uses based on contracts of agreements between the Child and the Parent ego states. For example:

1. To avoid guilt over an unfilled obligation

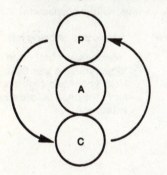

Child:	"I feel so sad."
Parent:	"Anyone as sad as you doesn't have to do what you promised you would do."

2. To indulge guilt-free in a denied pleasure

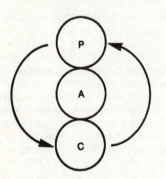

Child:	"I'm so scared."
Parent:	"Anyone as scared as you can wait for someone else to solve the problem." OR
Child:	"I'm mad!"
Parent:	"Anyone as mad as you has the right to break something."

3. To solicit a privilege

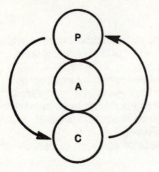

Child:	"I'm so tired."
Parent:	"Show people how tired you are. Anyone as tired as you has a right to expect other people to let you get in front of them in the grocery line."

4. To avoid a feeling which is seen as more dangerous, painful or shameful

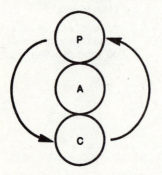

Child:	"I'm scared of being left."
Parent:	"Never say that! Don't forget you're a Van Dyke! Hold your head high and leave the bitch before she leaves you."

Feelings are muscular/chemical/electrical changes in the body. They represent a very vital self-protective mechanism in the face of danger to prepare one to fight or to run away. People who are in touch with their feelings are aware of these muscular-chemical-electrical changes in their bodies and may give them names, like *mad* or *scared* or *glad* or *sad*. A therapist can observe changes in posture, breathing, rate of speech, energy levels, etc. as evidence of "emotional" reaction. When people inhibit natural fight-flight reactions as a part of socialization, they use some muscles to react bodily and some to inhibit body reactions. Rackets are usually associated with muscular tensions and these tensions are usually available to the awareness. In plain talk, when I'm angry, I tense my forehead and stomach muscles instead of saying I'm angry or instead of blowing up. Or, when I'm sad, I pretend to be happy because my mother was so sad after my little brother died that I decided to be a little ray of sunshine to cheer her up. So now when I'm disappointed about something, I stay cheerful and appreciate what I *do* have.

Many people maintain a "turtle" posture with head sunken into their shoulders as though scared and self-protective, but they appear consciously unaware of such feelings. The blocked scared feeling shows in their muscles.

Most people who come to treatment groups arrive in pain. They hurt somewhere—head, neck, chest, shoulders, stomach, back—believing that it is better to tighten your body to tense up and hurt yourself, than to do something else. When very young, this may have been the best decision available.

Eric Berne said, "Think sphincter", to alert therapists to the muscular inhibitions to action and expression going on inside the patient. We count on the possibility that with information or permission, a person will change his behavior. Often, however, information or permission is not enough. There seems to be a belief, "If people know that I am angry, somthing very bad will happen. I will die, or everybody will go away, or my sick grandfather will die. Although these beliefs are not very reasonable or logical, a resourceful, bright person may find what sounds like very good reasons for inhibiting feeling expression. People usually use their intelligence to defend, perpetuate and justify their rackets, rather than to "smoke" them out. A racket feeling is usually supported and maintained by what the person is thinking and remembering.

Anger, sadness or fear involve a whole series of bodily changes. The person appraises the situation, and if he thinks "Watch out!" his pituitary gland signals the adrenal cortex which drops adrenalin into the blood. Intense heat or cold, x-rays, a cut or splinter, intense sound, pain, forced exercise or inhibition of movement almost always result in this syndrome: pituitary secretion, swelling and secretion of the adrenal cortex, ulceration of the stomach, shrinkage of the thymus, spleen, lymphatic organs and white blood cells (except that with heat the spleen enlarges). Selye calls this the syndrome of the response to injury. Such changes may be important factors in skin and other allergies, asthma, hay fever, arthritis, heart disease and other somatic illnesses. Persons subjected to fearful situations involving no tissue damage have reacted with bleeding ulcers. A scolding by a parent or boss may be such a fearful situation, or may arouse anger, which is quite different. Research by Wolff showed that in anger the stomach reddens, while in fear it turns pale. When a person suffers a loss or feels frustrated in not getting what he wants, he may or may not respond with the above syndrome.

A newspaper story tells of twenty miles of cars stopped for more than an hour bumper to bumper on the overseas highway to Key West because a bridge was out. Some people stormed or fumed, while others with a different appraisal organized a party, turned on their radios, danced, went skinny dipping, and had a party they would never forget. One person's reaction to frustration is different from another's.

When a person is aroused, the pupils of his eyes may dilate, his bowels get ready to evacuate, the heart beats faster, blood pressure rises, fingers get cold and palms wet. The person is all charged up to fight or to run away. This biological sequence is very likely several million years old. When a child becomes civilized at age 1, 2, 3, 4 etc., he learns to move his bowels only at certain times and places, he learns to fight or not to fight, or scream and run away.

Instead of energy flowing naturally through his body, he learns to block it here and there, and sometimes focuses so much on blocking that he does not have much energy available to solve his problems. He/she is afraid, "If I show how scared I am, my mother will make fun of me, or my father will not be proud of me, or he will be mad at my mother for babying me." Or, you name it.

A person who is sad day after day regardless of the situation is in a sad racket. This does not mean that she is a bad person or that she is trying to "trick" people. It means that she may be blocking another feeling, which, to her is even more dangerous. As unpleasant as it is to be sad, it might still seem better than to be angry. Or possibly, in her family, one had to be sad to get a "goody", and now being sad is the *tax* she must pay to her own internal Parent to justify some pleasures. Racket feelings are right out there where everyone can see them. They are easy to identify. By using the exercises below and some training, the hidden feelings can also easily be identified.

The first feeling we discuss is blocked fear.

Blocked Fear

The neck muscles are especially useful in diagnosing blocked feelings. We can observe the natural startle reaction of a newborn infant by dropping it a few inches or observing its reaction to a loud noise. The infant, when startled, draws his head back and throws out his arms. When an adult lies on his back on a firm mat and breathes deeply for 10-20 minutes, if we observe his head pulling back and his pupils dilating, we guess that he is having fear reactions and that his fears are not being expressed in his usual conscious waking and living state. He appears to be cool or angry when he is scared, instead of experiencing his fear or expressing it. (In fact, other people are often afraid in his presence.) And with the continued breathing and encouragement, he may express his fears, screaming, "I'm scared!" And he may recall an early scene when he was scared and decided it's better to be cool or angry than scared. If he recalls such a scene, we ask him to visualize it, think about it, talk about it, make a new decision— until he no longer has blocked energy in this area.

Blocked Grief

When she cries, the infant's head drops down on her chest. The muscles in the back of the neck are loose, those in front of the neck are tight. In the reclining and breathing exercise mentioned above, blocked sadness or grief is diagnosed by the hardening of the muscles at the front of the throat. A large lump in the throat may be seen or felt with the fingers. Massaging this bump and suggesting the person say repetitively, "I hurt" or "I'm sad" may help release the long-blocked sad feelings resulting in profound crying and grief for a few minutes followed by a big sigh of relief and joy. Persons who block feelings by talking and thinking may want to elaborate the "I hurt" and it is important if the energy is to go into the feeling, to gently suggest that the person limit her words to the repetitive simple phrase, "I hurt," or "I'm sad," or "I want my Mommy," or "It's too hard."

Blocked Anger

The person whose typical posture is scared, sad, or Mr. Cool, may be avoiding anger. Blocked anger becomes visible when the muscles going down the sides of the neck under the ears stand out in stunning relief, especially when the breathing exercise above is used. Massaging the tense muscles under the ears and encouraging angry shouts and pounding and kicking on the mat may release the blocked rage and allow the person to experience the possibility that it is O.K. to be openly angry.

Interlocking Rackets and Games

Fanita English has described the interlocking rackets of Helpless and Helpful. Helpless (who uses his sad or scared racket to avoid feeling his anger) looks for someone from whom to get help. Helpful (who uses her helpful loving racket to avoid facing her fear, anger or sadness) is looking for someone to help. Helpless secretly believes no one will really help the way Helpless wants to be helped any better than his not-O.K. parents did, and Helpful believes, "No matter how hard I try, in the end people won't be pleased with me. I'm really not O.K. and unloveable, but I try hard." So, Helpless and Helpful meet and they fall in love. Here is where the game develops. Helpful helps Helpless and in the beginning Helpless feels that at last he is getting what he wants, and Helpful believes that she is at last pleasing people and doing well. And then...one day Helpless says, "You're not doing it right." This confirms their original beliefs. So, they collect stamps, advance the script, structure time, and leave each other feeling bad (get the payoff). Nobody "hooks" anyone into interlocking rackets or games. People often like to disown their own parts in participating, and pretend to be "innocent bystanders" or victims of someone else's racketeering. (*Blaming* is a racket, too, and is seeing oneself as innocent, naive Victim.)

There are hundreds of such interlocking Rackets. To name a few: Smart Ass (but no one will ever really love me) and Stupid (I can't do it, but neither can you); I disappoint people (Ma wanted a boy, not me) and People disappoint me (You'll look good at first and then prove yourself a flash in the pan); Slave Driver and Drag Ass; Brave and Chicken; Feeler and Thinker; Worrier and Playboy.

Functional vs. Judgmental Approaches to Understanding Rackets

We may describe rackets functionally, investigating in what ways they have been of survival value to the racketeer or, we may see rackets as a way a person "tricks other people into feeling or doing for him." For a small child, his racket may be a way of surviving in that particular household. When he grows up and continues the racket behavior, it has no survival value, but it may enable him to establish contact and get strokes from people who have complementary rackets so that they can interlock (get symbiotic), and back to familiar feeling. If a person has decided or expects to feel sad (angry, scared, happy), he or she can feel that without all the preliminary events that have been contrived to justify the racket feeling. Willie comes into the room ready to feel a certain feeling, let's say sad to the fifth power, and only feels neutral. He says hello to no one in particular and someone answers "hello" in the perfunctory manner. Good! So now Willie feels sad first degree because 'They don't like me.' Someone says, "Pretty shirt you're wearing," and Willie answers, "This old thing? It's stained and has a hole in one sleeve and a button is missing... You just said that because you feel sorry for me." Sad, second degree. Thus, by selective perceptions he can get himself to feel sad, his old familiar place. This description does not see Willie as a sick, not-O.K., pathological or transactional criminal. It describes how he functions.

Therapy of Rackets

Since rackets involve beliefs, muscular tightness and blocked feelings, discarding rackets would require a person's understanding and appreciating the early survival value of the belief systems. The person would do well to learn the original and earlier survival value of his racket and appreciate its usefulness in childhood, rather than to attack this part of himself as bad. When a patient says, "I'd like to get rid of all this shit," we think they are less apt to change because they are not appreciating the usefulness of this maneuver to them in the past. Treatment groups offer opportunities to change behavior by getting strokes for expressing heretofore blocked feelings. Thus, if Joe has never expressed sad feelings and he begins to cry, we touch him or tell him we're glad that he is crying since he is so sad, or sit quietly with him.

One of the most powerful tools of the therapist is to withdraw. Withdrawing is an alternative to stroking the racket by extra sympathy, energy or persecution ("That sounds rackety to me.") When a patient is clearly in a racket, sometimes we leave the patient and go to someone else in the group for a few minutes. We come back to the patient later when he is ready to work.

Below is an exercise useful in small or large groups to help persons become aware of their muscular responses to rackety or rubberband feelings.

An Exercise to Relate Physical Tension to a Possible Racket

STEP ONE: To become aware of the muscle systems and tensions: Lie down, close your eyes, feel your body on the floor. (Pause 10 seconds before giving more directions.) Tighten your right fist, pull it tightly toward your right shoulder, bending your elbow, tighter, tighter...now relax. (Repeat the preceeding once again and do each of the following tensing and relaxing of a body part twice, pausing about ten seconds between each. Push out your left hand as tight as you can, push harder, still harder, now relax. Scrunch up your shoulders to your ears, higher, higher, now relax. Close your eyes very tight, tighter, tighter, now relax. Relax some more. Make a smile, a big smile. Bigger, so that your teeth show. Now relax. Stick out your tongue, farther, farther, now relax. Pull down your eyebrows. Pull them down even more. Now push them together so that you are trying to make the space between them disappear. Now relax. Pull your buttocks and sphincters together, as though you are avoiding an enema. Tighter, even tighter. Now relax. Take a very very deep breath and hold the air in. Feel the tension across your chest as you hold, now let the air out and feel yourself relax. Tense your stomach muscles as if someone were to punch you on the belly. Tighter, pulling your gut into the floor. Now relax. Point your right foot, like a toe dancer, harder, tighter, now relax. Push out your left heel and point the toe backwards toward your shoulder. Further, harder. Now relax. Now tense your whole body all at once. Ready, Tense. Tensing arms, fingers, stomach, eyes, mouth, feet, buttocks. Hold it and give it an extra tense. Ahhh, now relax. Take a deep breath.

STEP TWO: Relax your body. Feel the floor under you. Think of some recent unpleasant situation in your life. (Pause 1-2 minutes.) Notice your body sensations when you think about this situation. What tightened? (One minute pause.) Slowly open your eyes and look at the ceiling. (Pause 10 seconds.) Now look around the room, come back into the room. Sit up and look around. Find a partner and tell your partner what sensations you had, where you tensed yourself. (3 minutes.) Would someone tell the whole group where in your body you felt tense? "...In my neck..." O.K. Who else. (Give the group 3 to 10 minutes to speak of their experiences to the whole group. Leader doesn't analyze or give extensive comment about responses but rather receives them, hears and goes onto next comment.)

Rubberbands

The concept of rubberband feelings was first published in the Dave Kupfer Memorial Issue of the *Transactional Analysis Journal*, (Vol. 1, No. 2, 1971) by Dave Kupfer and Morris Haimowitz. A rubberband is any feeling in the Now that is turned on at occasions similar to some feeling-laden event in the past. Like feeling bad on September 18th and realizing that several September 18th's ago your best friend died. Sam walks into the treatment room where there are usually eight patients and two therapists, but on this occasion, two persons are absent. Sam says, "Where is everybody?" Since most of the people are here, the "Where is everybody?" is an overreaction, probably based on remains from some previous experience. Since he says, "Where is everybody?" when he sees two empty chairs, we know that empty chairs have a special meaning for Sam, different from most other people, and that is probably exciting him. So I say, "You see a couple of empty chairs and you have some feeling about it. Imagine you are little. What does an empty chair mean to you?" He replied, "When I was six years old, my father left us, and every night my mother set a place for him at the table, and his chair was always empty. He never came home." A rubberband is a feeling in the now plus an old feeling: $RB = FN + OF$.

The job of the therapist or facilitator is to use his intuition (Little Professor) to imagine what could make the person feel when she was five or ten years old what she feels now. The way the therapist does this is to imagine the patient as a child, to see this grown-up as a five-year-old, and the little kid comes in and says, "Where is everybody?" And then you get some pictures in your own head about what might have happened. This is different from a racket. It's only turned on at special times and is not usually a shakedown for strokes. It is a left-over, unfinished business which may have no secondary gain at all. Thus, a rub-berband feeling is an overreaction to a present situation.

Living people are full of feelings, constantly changing. And a person who is reactive is feeling what she is feeling at the moment and isn't bringing back a lot of stuff from the past. If a member of the group decides to leave the group and another member of the group says, "I feel bad. Everybody's leaving," it would be similar to the empty-chair rubberband. When I ask Beatrice to imagine her father in another chair and to talk to him and then to move into the other chair and be her father, and she says, "It's such a drag to move from this chair into the other chair. So I think, "What's the big drag about moving from a chair?" I imagine she's five years old, So I say, "Were you told as a child to stay in the chair like a good girl?" And she replies, "I was tied to a chair to make me eat."

Rubberbands or rackets can be happy, too. Some people have smiling rackets. Perhaps their parents told them to always smile and rewarded the smile. Even if they feel bad, they smile. Be a happy boy, be a sweet boy no matter what you're feeling. "Junior bluebirds are always brave and cheerful."

Sometimes the therapist guesses the rubberband or racket right on the head, and sometimes she misses completely, and the patient says, "No, that's not it," or "It wasn't that way; it was the other way around!..." etc. And in the end you're ahead for having guessed, even if you guess wrong because now Beatrice knows more about her reluctance to move.

Rubberbands can also enrich our lives. I walk under a tree and dew drops fall on my nose, and I remember playful Ivy spraying me with wet branches of a plum tree.

Stamps

People use trading stamps the way they use green stamps. You know how green stamps work—if you save one book of green stamps, then you can get a ballpoint pen. Or you could save fifty books and get a bicycle, and with a hundred books you can get a couch. Well, so it is that people save blue stamps. If Morris is supposed to meet me at three o'clock on the corner, and its cold, and he comes at three thirty, and he says, "Gee, I'm sorry, Nat," and I say, "That's O.K.," but maybe inside of me I'm feeling it's not O.K., instead of telling him how angry I am, I put a blue stamp in my book. I save a series of hurts with which to "buy" things. I could save a few hurts for a weekend drunk or depression. Or I could save for an affair, or I could save for a divorce or, with 5,000 books, for a suicide.

Now you know if you're saving stamps and you've almost enough and the A&P is giving double stamps that week, that's where you do your shopping. So, if I'm saving for a divorce, then I set up situations in which I'm sure to get hurts and amass more resentments. And when I get a little hurt, if I can feel twice as bad, it counts double.

Everyone in Ron's family was walking on eggs. Ron hadn't had a drink in six months and everyone was tense. His wife said, "What do you want for breakfast?" "Eggs," he said. "How would you like them?" she asked. "One over easy and one scrambled," he answered. His wife brought in the eggs. "Damn it!" he screamed, "You scrambled the wrong one!" Since she did it wrong, he now had enough stamps to get drunk.

Some people live out their scripts collecting hurt stamps. What we do in groups is to note the stamp collectors. If somebody in group verbally attacks another person in group, we encourage the person who has been attacked to give the other person back in kind, so it's over with. To borrow a term from scuba diving, it's a good idea to "blow as you go." The trouble with zealous stamp collectors is that when they cash in their blue stamps, they quietly sneak them back into their pockets (saving their resentments). So we work with a couple and the woman says, "I will never ever ever forgive you for how lousy you were when you left me and I had to take care of poor, sick Johnny all by myself." Then we say, "If you'll never forgive him, then there's no place to go in your marriage except out. Is there anything he could do that would make it up to you? What could make it even-Steven?" "Well," she might say, "if he would help me with the housework and take me on a long vacation..." So he helps her with the housework and they go on the long-awaited trip, and three months later he does something she doesn't like and she says, "...and besides, you let me suffer with poor, sick Johnny all by myself." So stamp collectors actively save hurts, and they fight cashing in the stamps, but rather borrow on them. Saving injustices is a way of life. Stamp collecting is saving up the cold pricklies until you have enough to do something harmful to yourself. Just what that is depends on your script, i.e., your early decision. It could be you're saving for a guilt-free divorce, or it could be you're planning on ending up in a tragic script—alone, sick, alcoholic, in prison, crazy. People collect blue stamps to buy "the blues"—something bad, or to have a script-attack.

Freud wrote hundreds of pages showing how hysterical symptoms, errors or mistakes in speech or action were ways of expressing repressed feelings. Freud immortalized Joseph Breuer for his great discovery that neurotic symptoms were re-enactments of forgotten traumatic experiences and might be cured by hypnosis and re-living the repressed event. Freud's concept of abreaction: which means to re-act or discharge repressed thoughts or feelings is father to the idea of rubberbands. We use these ideas frequently in group therapy. For example:

Sarah: I'm angry at Fred for putting down the governor. I know he just wants to be friendly but I get very angry when he puts someone down.
Therapists: When you were little who in your family put people down? (We are looking for the rubberband.)
Sarah: My mother. She put down my father.
Therapist: Let's hear how she did it. (Sarah then acts out the very emotional scene.)

VIII. Scripts

We think of a script as a plan of action, a map of one's life which is inflexible, relentlessly predictable, almost unchangeable throughout life, involving pain, suffering or boredom, made consciously between the ages of 3 and 12 by a child in a stressful situation. When Alfred Adler was writing around 1900 he was aware of inflexible life plans and he wrote much about them calling them life styles. Scripts come in all shapes and sizes. Some are short and sweet like Cinderella and some are long and bitter like Anna Karenina. Each of us is our own script writer. We make a life plan including what we expect to happen to us, who plays important roles and how's it going to come out in the end. Some people like to believe that bad things have just happened to them, and bad people have just happened along. We don't believe that. We believe that like a producer of a play, we also cast the parts in our play.

Suppose you are casting a play for Red Riding Hood. You need a Little Red, a wolf, grandma, a hunter. And if your life script is like Little Red's, you could be looking around for a wolf, grandma, etc. You meet Mr. Charming. He arrives on time and brings you roses. He will never make it as the wolf. Drop him. Then you meet Mr. Rascal. He shows up an hour late, forgets the tickets, borrows money from you and leaves in your car for some personal emergency. Wow! He is exciting. I may not be aware of it, but I'm looking for a wolf to do me in. My mother believed men were no damned good, only interested in one thing, and I decided Mom was right. She often told me what a louse Dad was. If this wolf gets away, I'll grab the next wolfish person I can lay my hands on. The man who plays "wolf" in my play is also casting his play. Maybe he has decided as a lad that women look innocent, seducing you and then do you in, just like his mother did when she ratted on Dad to the IRS. He's looking for a sweet, innocent, docile woman to play the role of temptress in his life. They meet and fall in love and both use each other to play out their dramas, proving what they decided as little children, and thinking "If it weren't for you, things would be better."

Script Decisions

The important script messages, then, are from the Adapted Child of mother and dad, usually in the form of rewards (added strokes, energy, love, contact) and punishment (withdrawal, withholding of strokes, threatened abandonment.) Script decision theory follows stroke theory. Since children need strokes to survive, giving or withholding strokes has a very powerful impact on each of our lives. For example, the child runs in flashing a beautiful report card. Daddy turns

58

around, without a word, and walks out of the room. What does the child make of this? What is father saying, not by his words, but by his acts? Don't show off? Don't be important? If father walks out for a good report card, what does father pay attention to? A rash? A broken leg? A little asthma? So the child's little professor may think, "If I'm going to make it around here I better get sick or break a leg." And the kid shows up frequently sick or "accident prone." Note the father never said "You should break a leg." The script decision is made by the child based on whatever limited information he has and based on his sensitivity to the stroke economy of the moment. Like Berne's patient mentioned on page 66.

Here are some examples of script decisions:

People will hurt me. I'll hurt them first, fighting everyone in my way.

I'm powerful. I have to be silent, stoney and passive so as not to hurt people.

Something is wrong with me. If I'm real nice to people, maybe no one will notice how bad I am.

If I'm not in charge of everything, something terrible will happen.

No one will help me unless I'm sick or sad.

No man will ever love me. But I'll try to please them anyway.

Women are stupid. I can't expect anything from a woman except cooking, washing and sex.

The only thing I can do when I feel bad is take drugs or booze.

I'm special. I have great talent and promise; so ordinary living is ------.

I'll never show anyone or tell anyone how I feel or what I want.

I'll work hard and produce but I'll end up disappointed.

If I'm not careful people will take advantage of me.

If I'm mean to you and you like me, I'll think you're a fool.

If I'm mean to you and you are mean to me, then I'll be nice to you until I get even.

The No-No's (Injunctions)

Bob and Mary Goulding's work on script injunctions won them the Eric Berne Memorial Award in 1975. Essential to the script decision which is made by the Child are the injunctions, or no-no's—messages given by the parents not so much in words as in behavior, such as feeding, dressing, or bathing the infant roughly, ignoring the infant's pain, walking away or over-reacting when the kid comes in with a sad story or a bloody knee.

These are the most important injunctions:

Don't Be messages come from the parents, whose suffering is so intense they think of killing themselves, and they are so preoccupied with their own pain that they ignore the needs of the infant. A child may cry for hours before being attended to. So the infant grows up thinking "I'll never get what I need; I'm a burden to people; I can help them by killing myself."

Don't Feel means don't laugh or cry or be angry or scared because when you do Mom leaves the room. Such people grow up addicted. When they get a feeling, they suppress it with booze, drugs, food, or work.

Don't Think messages may come from a father who doesn't want his son to be smarter than he. Usually, this father was an oldest child who felt abandoned when a younger brother or sister appeared. Or these messages might come from a mother who felt anxious if the child were smart—he might know about her flirtation with the milkman, or about Aunt Suzy being crazy. As long as David acted stupid, mother felt safe. Sometimes the message is given lovingly, "If his head weren't screwed onto his body, he'd lose that too, ha, ha," implying that David is lovable, confused and "we love you that way."

Don't Grow Up ideas get sent by a parent who loves infants but not big kids, or by parents who say it's so hard to be a grown up. So the child decides it's better not to grow up. Laurie (age 27) can't finish her term paper or degree or get married; Ned (age 9) can't tie his shoelaces yet because when he ties them, Mom says, "You can't do it right," and ties them for him. Their favorite fairy tale is *Peter Pan.*

Don't Be A Child comes from parents who act helpless and confused and want to be children and want the infant to take care of them. So by the time Dale was two, he was already washing the dishes and sweeping the floor. He's not supposed to play and have fun. If Mom is feeling bad, Dale will be there with a hot water bottle, aspirin, and a cup of tea. When Dale grows up he will be handy around people who need comforting. If someone is crying, Dale will rush tearfully to her aid.

Don't Be Who You Are. We wanted a boy and a girl. Instead, we got a boy and a boy. So Bob was supposed to be Bobette, and he wore dresses instead of pants. Between the ages of twenty to thirty, he couldn't decide whether to be a lawyer or accountant, and he had trouble deciding whether he wanted strawberry or chocolate ice cream on his pie. Trouble in deciding often means "Am I male or female?" Parents may have wanted a tall thin child instead of a short fat one, or a light skinned instead of a dark skinned, or an engineer, not a pianist. No matter what the kid does, he or she feels "I am not right," and diets, has a nose job or a breast or penis job to please some parent longings, but in vain.

Don't Be Close. Don't touch Mommy! Your hands are dirty! Don't talk to me about your pain and troubles, I'll get scared. And so Darlene never quite gets married, or if she does, maintains a cool distance from her husband and children.

Don't Be Important. Parents may give the message very quickly, "I'm the important one around here; you are not important and don't forget it." So when Eddie gets to be captain of the Little Leaguers and when Sarah is made President of the PTA, they flub it, become tongue-tied. Sarah can serve the tea and Eddie can be water boy. No sweat.

Attributes

Along with the No-No's (usually non-verbal) another important source of scripting are verbalized descriptions of how the child supposedly is, along with lots of stories about him that supposedly occurred before he could remember. These are offered with humor, affection and admiration (from Mommy's and Daddy's Child) which makes them insidious, such as:

Roger is so interested in nature that when I send him to the store he looks at birds and usually gets lost. (This supports a *Don't Think* injunction.)

Mary had such a grown up head on her shoulders she always looked like a little old lady. (Supports *Don't Be A Child.)*

He's a real thrill seeker. Always has been. He was hitching rides on freight cars when he was five years old. He fell off the roof and broke his arm when he was six. He could ride a motorcycle when he was ten. (Supports a *Don't Be* injunction.)

George is such a barrel of fun. You can always count on him to do something crazy, all wrong. And fun—he's a riot! (Supports *Don't Grow Up.)*

As a baby, you were no trouble at all. We could put you to sleep anywhere, even on the floor and you would sleep. You would eat anything we gave you. It was as though there were no baby in the house. It was a pleasure to have you. (Supports a *Don't Be Important* injunction.)

Larry was so independent. Even as a baby he refused to let me hold him or feed him. He insisted on holding his own bottle. (Supports a *Don't Get Close* injunction.)

In treatment groups, people overcome the injunctions by being asked to violate them in the group (Be Important; Feel; Think; Be Who You Are; Enjoy Yourself . . .) and reinforcing the new behavior by giving strokes. Sometimes the new behavior is so fearful that therapy proceeds from finding out how and when in-injunctions were given and then making new life decisions before changing the behavior. Strokes given for changed behavior may be a simple, "Yes," or "Good" or pat on the back, handshake, or when a really big change is seen, a group massage.

Counterscripts

Counterscripts are more conventional messages to succeed which usually come verbally from Mommy's or Daddy's Parent. "You should study diligently, work hard, finish everything on your plate, early to bed, early to rise, earn a lot of money, make friends, be a man, be important, tell the truth." Counterscripts are based on "Do's" from Mommy's or Daddy's Parent to Jimmy's or Mary's Parent, and often they are in conflict with the script injunctions given from Mommy's and Daddy's Child to the son or daughter's Child. The mixed message would be like this: While Mrs. Columbus is telling Christopher verbally, "Stay home, Christopher," with her Child she might be giving him strong non-verbal "Get lost" or "It's dull here," or "Go discover America" messages.

Most kids who drop out of school are getting mixed messages from the grown-ups around them. The grown-ups are saying, "You should stay in school," but the powerful messages from the grown-ups' Child are, "Get out of here, you troublemaker," or from the pupil's parent's Child are, "Don't waste time in school; go out and make money." Remember Berne's third law of communication, that when there are duplex transactions, the messages coming from the Child will have much more impact than those coming from the Adult or Parent.

Therapists have to be very careful about figuring out what the script is and what the counterscript is because what looks like a burdensome counterscript (work eighteen hours a day and make no mistakes) might actually be better than the script (don't be). And if the therapist pushes the person to give up his counterscript, the person might start taking big chances with his life, i.e., driving drunk, provoking people who have a chip on their shoulder, etc. In the early days of TA, we were intoxicated with heavy Parent stuff and encouraged patients to turn off their Parent (work only eight hours a day), and patients became very uneasy and what they turned to were early messages: "Who needs you? Scram! Drop Dead!"

Since then, therapists have learned it's not a good idea to turn off the Parent messages until the patient learns new ways to get lots of strokes for his Child. If there are any suicidal or near-winner or loser script messages, they would be in the patient's Adapted Child, which may be clarified by having the patient tell his favorite fairy tale. In other words, maybe my mother said, "Wait until the right man comes along," so I'm waiting, I'm four years old, and I'm thinking, "Wait, wait, wait," and I wonder how I can solve my problems. One day I read *Sleeping Beauty* and I think, "Say, that's a beautiful story. I could solve my problems like Sleeping Beauty." Children pick a fairy tale character that seems to be living a story just like theirs, and they get mixed up with the fairy tale character. One of Claude Steiner's gifts to TA showed how the child received script and counterscript messages from his parents. For this Steiner was awarded the first Eric Berne Memorial Award in 1971. Here are some speculations of Columbus' script matrix:

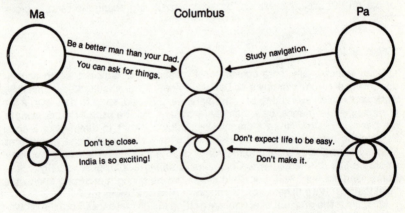

Some Possible Messages from the Parents of Columbus

You remember Rumpelstiltskin, who tricked a country maiden to convert hay into gold. So the person with the Rumplestiltskin script might think she has to take worthless garbage and make it into jewels or, like Henry Higgins, find some little scrap of nobody and make her into a lady. This could be taught by some early Parent messages that say, "Don't want much, don't take much, don't waste anything. Look how smart she is! She wove a beautiful rug out of old rags."

Sometimes parents give kids contradictory messages: "Get it done fast—but don't speed;" "Be brave—be obedient." When your patient is a policeman who is really going hard after those crooks, perhaps his script is to be a crook, and his counterscript is to catch crooks. An alcoholic may stop drinking by going out to save other alcoholics. His counterscript is to save alcoholics. The script is to be an alcoholic. If he stopped saving alcoholics, he might have to be an alcoholic. Berne talked about all the reformed alcoholics in a little town who decided that they were going to save all the alcoholics. So they formed an Alcoholics Anonymous club. When everybody in town who was an alcoholic belonged to the association, there was nobody left to save. They had nothing left to do but start drinking again.

There are a few basic kinds of scripts. "Don't Get Close" is a very common one. You find people who are lonely and by themselves or who can't stay with their husbands or who can't find girlfriends. Mom is unhappy with her husband and tells her daughter that men are no damn good. "Look at what a bastard your father is." So daughter finds one husband after another who is no good—proving her mother was right. Another common script is "To Be A Failure, Be A Loser."

Claude Steiner tells us the script decision usually is made at a time of punishment or disappointment with great pain or excitement. A kid is spanked for doing something wrong or someone tells him, "You'll never amount to anything, you little . . ." or "Look at what a crazy fool you are, ha, ha."

The little girl is given permission by her father to grow up and become a woman (having fun, joking, dressing, stroking, nurturing, grooming, dating, cooking). The little boy is given permission by his mother to grow up and become a man, and his daddy shows him how (cooking, dressing, dating, working, stroking, nurturing, having fun). Sometimes the parent of the opposite sex gives messages *not* to grow up, and the parent of the same sex shows the child how to stay a kid. Suppose the little boy sleeps with his mommy until he is eighteen years old. This is not giving him permission to be a man. Usually in this situation his daddy is not around much to show him how, or dad acts like a little boy himself, like one who can't take care of himself. So the kid doesn't have a good chance of growing up and becoming a man the way we think of a man. Both parents are involved in the script messages, either actively, on the scene, by what they do and how they live, or by not being there and giving messages about how it's O.K. to cop out and run away.

Some parents have an urgent need to say, "I have a daughter" when they have a son, or, "I wish I had a son" when they have a daughter. Or they give the girl a boy's name like Randi or Jeri. Or they dress a boy child in girl's clothing and let his hair grow in a fashion common for girl children. Or they call a boy a "tomboy," a term usually used for girls who are physically active. The son or daughter is getting the message: "Don't be what you are; if only you were the other kind."

People who have grown up with such messages often seize on one aspect of their physical self which they begin to feel is "all wrong." The boy might think, "If I were only 3 inches taller, then I could be an O.K. man." Or, "If I only didn't have a nose like I have." The girl might think, "If I only were ten pounds thinner," or "If I only had a bigger bosom or a smaller bosom, then I would be O.K." Usually the conflict about having been born the wrong sex is later experienced around some other unchangeable physical characteristic: "Why did I have to be so tall?"

Identification of Scripts

How do we identify one's life script? Sometimes this is done by observing the person's present situation. If he has been divorced three times, he probably has made a script decision not to trust women, or to stay lonely; if he has been arrested several times, he probably has made some decision to fight society or end up in jail. If he drinks excessively, he may have decided, before age twelve, he would end up a drunkard. If he has threatened or attempted suicide, the decision might have been to kill himself.

Sometimes present behavior does not give a clear clue as to life plan, and perhaps there is no script. We can ask a few of the questions below which may help in unraveling a script: What are your favorite TV shows, comic strips? When you were a child, what were your favorite stories or fairy tales? Tell us the story. Whom in it do you like and dislike? How are you like those persons? What is the magic part of the story? What kind of magic are you expecting in your life? What is the worst thing your parents ever said to you—or about you? And what was the nicest thing they ever said to you? What was a typical statement your mother made about life? Your father? What did they want you to do? Describe them. When did your parents pay most attention to you—when you were sick, when you did well, when you were in trouble? How did you tease or excite them? What will you be doing in the next five or ten years? How long will you live? What will it say on your tombstone? Draw a picture of your family doing something together when you were little. You are in the picture.

Robert (age 47) told me, "The worst thing my father ever said was to his brother about me. He said, 'Bobby is the smartest boy in school. He can fix his wagon; he can do anything.'"

"Why was that the worst thing?"

"Because it meant he would never help me anymore."

"What did you think?"

"I decided I would have to do everything for myself and mustn't ask him anymore, and I was six years old and scared of dogs on the way to school."

"Your father said you were a smart boy, and that was the worst thing he ever said to you?"

"Yes, he said it lots of times to his brothers."

We see here how the child takes a statement from his parent and makes his own life plan from it. Possibly Robert was reading his father accurately: When Dad said, "You're smart," he meant "I don't want to help you." And possibly Robert got it mixed up: When Dad said, "You're smart," maybe he meant, "I'm proud of you." We write this to show that the *child* makes the script decision based on messages from the parent. The parent does not script the child.

Script decisions may be observed by behavior in the group. Does she choose life and "action" or wait to be chosen? Does she take the initiative or sit in a corner? Does she play kick me, good guy, schlemiel, harried or NIGYSOB?

A child gets thousands of messages from his parents, but for some reasons not clear to us at this time, recalls only certain ones relating to his life plan. Parents give many messages, but the child makes the script decision. Sometimes the parent says something like this, "Why don't you brush your teeth?" and the kid says to herself, "Yea, why don't I brush my teeth? I wonder why I don't brush my teeth." This is not a clear message that "You should brush your teeth." The message is, "Something's wrong with you. Let's talk about how you're not O.K." Even a clear message may carry contradictory overtones: "Don't put this bean in your ear" puts an idea in the kid's head about where to put the bean that he never thought of before.

Claude Steiner, who worked with alcoholics, says that most of the people who come to him have never been told by anyone, "Don't drink!" Instead, people say, "Why do you drink?" and "Why do you make things miserable for yourself?" but no one has ever said, "Don't drink." Mommy says to little Sally, "If you don't clean your room, you won't get to watch television." What that is telling her is, "Go ahead and don't clean your room, and we can have fun later arguing about the television. Because if I say to you, 'Don't do this,' and if you do it, let me tell you what happens next! I'm already having fantasies that you're not going to do it and we're going to go for the $64 prize." So if parents say to their kids, "Do this" or "Don't do that," that's simple and straightforward.

Eric Berne told this story: The mother goes into the kid's room at 7:30, and he's watching television. Mother says to the kid, "Hey, why don't you do your homework?" And the kid says, "Let me just watch the end of this program." So the mom says, "O.K." An hour later she comes back and he's still watching television. This time her decibels go up. She makes more noise and she says, "Hey! You're not doing your homework! You said you were going to stop and do your homework when the program was over!" (see, he's getting a lot of strokes) and he says, "O.K., I'll do it, I'll do it!" An hour later she comes in and it's getting to be ten o'clock and the kid's still watching television and no homework's been done and she screams at him and he screams at her and they have a big fight and she slams the door and he slams the door and you know he's not going to study that night. What happens the next day? She goes and sees the principal of the school and calls her clergyman and gets in touch with her psychiatrist and tells the mothers at the PTA meeting how bad the schools are these days what with giving the kids too much (little) homework and how bad TV sets are. So she got a lot of energy, excitement and strokes out of this. If the kid had just done his homework, the whole night and the next day would have been dull and boring. The message to the kid is to go ahead and get in trouble, it makes life interesting for (the little girl in) Mom. The more boring Mom's life is, the more her Child is going to need excitement. This kind of fight is not pleasant for either participant; but it is exciting and produces an energy "turn on" for both.

Gene decided he was not important at age 2 when his father and mother split and his mother left Gene with a sixteen-year-old aunt while Mom went to work. By age 9, his aunt had left too, and Gene was fat and surly. One morning he phoned his Mom at work to say he couldn't find his house key. Since his Mom went off to work at 6:00 a.m., he always made his own breakfast, took his key, and went off to school. Mom wasn't supposed to spend time on the phone while at work, so she was very curt, "I don't know where your key is! Look in your coat pocket! Good bye!" Gene went off to school wondering how he would get in. It was very cold outside. He didn't hear the teacher's story about the Eskimos, and all of his behavior that day (losing his key, calling Ma at work—she had said, "Don't call me, see your teacher or Mrs. Jones next door if you need something"—not talking to Mrs. Jones and not seeing his teacher, and thinking how bad everything is) confirmed his basic position: "I'm not O.K., I'm not important and no one will care about me."

Gallows Laugh. Sometimes we get clues about a script from a gallows laugh, a ha ha associated with pain or misfortune. I lost my job, haha. The haha is not from pleasure. It may be a confirmation of a decision made much earlier that life would be painful. Freud, a prolific writer about humor, wrote in his Collected Papers "Humour," 1928 ". . . a criminal being led to the gallows on a Monday observes, 'Well, this is a good way to begin the week.' " Transactional Analysts believe the gallows laugh confirms an early painful script decision.

We were privileged to watch Eric Berne lead his treatment group in 1967 and noticed him attend to a little ha ha when a patient mentioned the possibility of having an auto accident. "What's the ha ha for?" he asked very softly. She said, "Well, if I get hurt in an accident, I would be helpless and busted up. I'd need someone to take care of me. I would have to go to my father and stepmother's house." Berne said, "If you want your father and stepmother to take care of you, could you visit them without an automobile accident?" We might guess that her script decision was "The only way I can get any attention is to get hurt."

Taibi Kahler in his miniscript theory has made an important contribution, finding a brief way to sample small segments of behavior and from them to understand and diagnose how people live out their scripts on a day-to-day basis in their speech, posture and general behavior. A brilliant contribution to script theory was made by Fanita English. She called the process of transmitting scripts from person to person "Episcript," pointing out how a person, having made a self-destructive decision may pass it, like a "hot potato," to someone else to live it out.

IX. Transactional Analysis Group Treatment

Contracts

Transactional analysis is contractual therapy; that is, clear agreements are made between the patient (or problem solver) and therapist (or facilitator).

There are two parts to the contracts: *The Business Contract* in which both parties agree as to time, place, fees. If the time is 9 to 11 a.m., this means the business of both parties will be 9 to 11 a.m.—not 9:10 or 9:15 until someone wants to stop. If the therapist works for someone else, in a hospital, jail, clinic, or office, then the therapist has an agreement with the boss about time, place, kinds of therapy permitted, rules, what will be permitted and what is against the rules. Establishing the mutually agreed upon rules as public information is for everyone's protection.

For Berne, the contract was also that the patient (problem solver) would show examples of his behavior, and the therapist (facilitator) agrees to be "a keen observer, thoughtful listener, curious investigator, disciplined clinician, meticulous technician, a conscientious physician, and an independent thinker."*

The Treatment Contract (or what is the problem to be solved?). A good contract includes feeling, thinking, acting. "Why are you here?" we ask. If the problem-solver says, "Because my mother sent me," or "My husband (or wife) sent me," then we say, "O.K., you say you're here because someone sent you. So now that you're here, what do you want to change in your life?" If we get, "I'm only here because someone sent me," or "She says I'm to do thus and so," we do not have a contract, and we say, "The chances of your changing something because someone else wants you to are slim." Persons usually come to the group because they feel deep pain which is powerful motivation to change their behavior.

We have several rules about good contracts, that is, contracts which are likely to be carried out. First, the contract is made with all three ego states. The patient's Parent says the desired behavior is moral, legal and ethical. If everyone else in the group feels it is moral, but the patient's Parent does not, we may build in a new Parent. Thus, if a person wants to be able to play and does not because Parent says that is bad, we build in a new Parent who says play is good. The Adult says the desired behavior is possible and safe. The Child says the behavior

---

*Berne's description of Karl Abraham, "who exhibited all the qualities a good therapist should strive for." Eric Berne, PRINCIPLES OF GROUP TREATMENT, p. 99 (New York: Grove Press, 1970).

is fun or interesting. So, if all parts of the patient say GO, we feel we have a good contract. Some examples of a good contract: breathe deeply for two minutes; speak to three people in the group; ask two people for something you want. If a person says, "I want to realize my potentials," or "be more productive" or "grow," we may say "That sounds like a mental health text book." If a woman says she wants to communicate better with her husband, we know that communicate is not a Child word, and the problem with many marriages is that the wife and husband are communicating—doing the RIGHT thing—but not enjoying each other. If the Child will feel better if the contract is carried out, and her Adult is thinking about ways to make it happen, and the Parent says, "Good! Go to it," then we agree to the contract. The new behavior which the group is supporting is often its own reward, although it might feel strange and exciting or frightening at first. The contract is to change the person's own behavior, not his parents', children's or wife's. We get a treatment contract as soon as possible, which means in five minutes, or in the second or third week.

Another rule is that the behavior to be changed is observable. X says, "I want to do what I'm doing, but I want to feel better." Not a good contract. Chances are, if you do what you have been doing, you will feel what you have been feeling. So if you want to laugh or scream and don't usually do that, and we can see you laughing or screaming, that is an observable behavior change.

In treatment, people usually work on painful experiences, and sad feelings. The group usually sympathizes, but not for very long if a person is prolonging his suffering because he got lots of strokes for suffering as a child. We intend for the group to be an exciting and fun place. Humor is a peculiarly human healthy activity.

Another rule in making contracts is to start something, not to stop something. We don't usually make a contract to stop smoking, drinking, eating, fighting unless we also make a contract to start talking, looking at people, phoning, jumping, riding a bike, asking, or 100 other acts. To stop something without replacing it leaves a vacuum in the time structure. When a person starts thinking about new activities, he spends less time smoking, drinking, eating, etc.

Another rule is that contracts are here and now, short term. For persons who look at the floor or ceiling, a good contract might be to look at other people in the group; for those who never touch, we may contract to touch; for those who never cry or express anger or fear, we contract to visibly and audibly express feelings, to cry when sad, to shout when angry, or to cringe or shake when scared. Long-term contracts, to get married or get a degree, are O.K., but less useful than seeing behavior change here and now. Next week a new contract may be made, or an old contract may be renewed.

Finally, we have a rule about how long we will work with one person. In a two-hour group, if we have eight members, we usually work with each person about 15 minutes. Sometimes we work only two or three minutes, and sometimes twenty, and rarely thirty minutes with one person. Often, there is a good deal of group participation and we work less with individual members.

Contracts with Suicidal or Alcoholic Patients

When a person understands her script—a process which may take five minutes or five years—she can take steps to change it. With drinkers and people who want to commit suicide, therapists say directly, "Don't drink," or "Don't commit suicide." In fact we make a contract with the person that under no circumstances will she hurt herself, directly or indirectly. "We care about you. We want a contract that you will be compassionate with yourself, be good to yourself." We make a contract to live, to enjoy being alive. Sometimes we ask the patient for a contract not to drink for a week. And the next week she makes a new contract not to drink. Some therapists ask for a contract that the patient take antibuse. She sees a doctor to get a prescription for antibuse, which makes her sick if she drinks. The therapist says, "Did you take your antibuse this week?" and if the patient says, "Yea," and winks or giggles, that wink means that she didn't take it all the time or she's not doing something right. Dr. Frank Ernst says if she is looking at you with her head and her eyes cocked at an angle, there is something not straight going on. She's not on the level. She's got an angle.

Most people who drink are not aware of their feelings. For example, the little kid is crying because she wanted something that her mother said she couldn't have, and Mommy says, "You're not angry, you're just tired." Or the kid says, "I hate my sister," and Mom says, "You don't hate your sister, you love your sister." So the kid has a strong message to be confused about her feelings, not to feel what she feels or not to reveal what she feels—first to Mom and then to herself. When she starts to feel, it is so frightening she says, "If I don't have this drink, I'll go crazy." We tell her, "Don't drink. You won't go crazy." Some people who drink believe that their mad is madder than other people's mad. They're so afraid of their feelings they live as if once that genie, my feelings, get out of the bottle, I'll never get them back in and under control. So they hold back and make their lives drab except when they're drinking, at which time they liven things up, express themselves, and let go, along with a lot of not O.K., self-destructive stuff. Often people who drink too much do things when they are drunk that they don't do when sober: feel sad, angry, joyful, enthusiastic, etc.

Sometimes people get others to live out their scripts in their places. Everybody knows about stage mothers. They are ladies who were supposed to be ballerinas or actresses and didn't quite make it. So they're stroking their kids for performing and telling their kids how talented they are and how they have to put their talent first before everything else. Parents who keep telling a kid that he's crazy have crazy on their minds, very likely because they are scripted to go crazy from messages like this: "That kid of ours sure is crazy, ha, ha," or "Why do you always have to be crazy?" or "You're driving me crazy." Instead of going crazy, the parent gets somebody else to go crazy, like a hot potato that is tossed around. The episcript, described by Fanita English, is the script transferred to someone else "hot potato" style. When therapists work with families, there's one Identified Patient in the family. That means one person in the family is conspicuously in trouble and the rest of the family looks O.K., well, successful and symptom-free. And the family says, "We've come to find out how to help poor messed-up Sally." The parents usually balk at the idea that somehow they have lots to do with what's going on with Sally. What's dramatic is that if the family can get rid of Sally, if somebody else becomes the IP**, this is a sign that something is going on with the parents, that they need somebody to act crazy.* So they choose a favorite child to be crazy, and if this child goes, the parents may get to what's cooking with them or they may find a replacement for Sally, any family member to show symptoms.

This is a possibility in the treatment relationship, too. Without being aware of it, some professionals get their patients to fight for them, stray for them, divorce instead of them, and so on. We insist that therapy be part of a TA therapist's training, with lots of soul-searching, so that therapists are not using patients to get themselves off a crazy hook or some other kind of hook (script).

Some patients are scripted to be the best. The patient comes to see a therapist and says he wants to live in a more leisurely fashion, but he just doesn't

Family Pie—Attributes

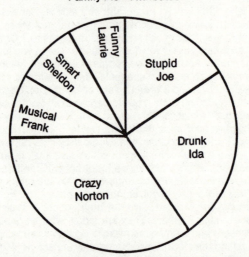

Sheldon's family had an attribute or expectation for each member, along with a standard for how much reward in family interest and attention would go with each. In Sheldon's family much more interest and attention went with being crazy than with being funny. In family systems each role (piece of the pie) must be maintained. If Ida stops getting drunk someone else starts. If Ida stays drunk till she dies, the next baby in the family may be named Ida and slated for that job in the family.

---

*Virginia Satir, CONJOINT FAMILY THERAPY.
**IP is Identified Patient. The one in the family who's supposed to be not O.K.

seem to be able to do it. He attracts work and does a good job, and then more is offered to him, and the first thing you know he's snowed under again and working his head off to dig his way out. What are our hunches? Maybe Daddy said, "You should do everything moderately," but he was really excited when the kid was best. The kid makes a decision, whether to go with the script (be best) or the counterscript (take it easy). Or maybe Daddy said, "Be the best, or don't be."

If a patient comes in and says, "I'm a lawyer, and I've got a good practice, but every time I take a new case I get very scared and I have the feeling that it could all go splash. Like a house of cards. In two minutes it could all fall down. I know I've got something solid, I built it up all these years, but there's a part of me that feels I'm going to lose everything. Every time I get an opportunity, I experience it as a potential disaster." So I as therapist am thinking, "His Child keeps hearing script messages like, 'Screw it up,' so he is urgently sticking to a counterscript, sticking with his Parent messages about what he *should* do. He works very rigidly, is very compulsive, is afraid of anything new, is meticulous, because he feels 'One false move and it's over.'" So I as therapist, am pretty sure he is working in a counterscript, and I ask him to continue being meticulous while examining the origins of his "Be best but screw up" messages. Except for the don't drink (or take drugs) and don't commit suicide contracts, I do not ask patients to make big changes in their lives outside the group. If they make changes, it's because they want to, not because we ask them to.

The therapist's job is to work on the patient's problem as stated in the contract. So, contracts can be made in a few minutes: I'll look people in the eye—right now, I'll react to what's going on here and now. The therapist is expected to work on the contract, not on other things. The therapist might say, "Hey, I see something else—you want to work on that?" If the patient agrees, they make a new contract. Sometimes it takes weeks to get a contract. Treatment without a verbalized contract is less likely to be successful. Sometimes we see people working, working, working, and we don't know what they're going to change in their behavior, so we ask the therapist in our training program, "What's her contract?" or "What is she working on?"

The therapist works with each individual person to fulfill her contract in the group. We're talking about group therapy, since group therapy appears to be much more powerful and effective than individual therapy for most people because the therapist can see how the patient behaves with other people and the group provides patients with an easy and sure source of strokes. The therapist isn't as confined in a group as she is with individual patients. She can work with a patient briefly and move on and spend lots of time with another patient who is ripe for change at this moment. She works in a group, but she talks to individual patients in the group. Her job is to help cure each of the patients of her problems in this session. When Berne did not cure people immediately, he said it was for one of four reasons: 1. I didn't use clear, simple language. If I use complicated language, how is he going to understand what I'm saying? 2. I talked too much. If I talk too much, how can he hear it all? 3. I didn't give him permission to get well. Some patients don't get well because the therapist doesn't want them to get well. 4. I was not potent. The therapist must be more potent than the crazy messages in the patient's head.

Awareness In TA Therapists

What good therapists or facilitators do is learn to re-experience with that part of us called the Little Professor, so that we can tune in to the people we work with and attend to them more with our senses than by listening to the words they speak. When we work with people, we do best when we blot out language and guess about what is happening and what is about to happen. If you do that a lot, and check it out, you'll be surprised how right you become because what you are doing is giving yourself permission to do something you did very well when you were nine months old. Without reason or words, this part of you knew what was going on.

Sometime before a child develops language ability, she begins to be aware of what makes her comfortable or uncomfortable. For example, when taken to a pediatrician's office for some reason, a baby knows the smells and sounds, and the baby starts crying, somehow sensing it's shot-time-minus-four-minutes. How does the baby know? It isn't words because the baby doesn't know any words yet. Before the child knows language, she uses senses to know whether she is safe or in danger. How come a kid doesn't go to sleep the night his parents are having a party? How does the baby know something is up? It's not language but rather the baby possibly getting a cue from how it feels to be around a hurried Mommy—her breathing is different, her movements are different. We're talking about an intelligence that is pre-language, based on the senses. What happens when a child looks at a bird and mother says, "Honey, that's a bluebird," is that less of his energy goes into experiencing the bird, and more of his energy goes into remembering that that creature is a bluebird; and still later, the experience of the bluebird is even more diluted when the child gets strokes for being able to spell "bluebird."

When we think of what qualities make for a good therapist, one is having a good Little Professor, that is, for the therapist to have permission to experience, to see, hear, taste, feel, smell, fantasize, and guess. Another is having permission to cure people. And the most important is to see people as O.K. If you have some need to see people hurt (maybe your own Child is still angry about things that happened to you once upon a time), you'll use your Little Professor to help people along the road to disaster. (There are some therapists who urge their patients to act crazy or take risks, *i.e.,* stroke them for taking the therapist's own "hot potato"). Some therapists do this by saying "Wowie!" when their patient says "I overdosed twice last week, or fell off a cliff, or took an LSD trip, or rode my bike 100 mph or found a friend who would leave me, or got drunk again, ha, ha." Good therapists puts lots of energy into finishing up their own "unfinished business" of the past so that this will not happen. A therapist who has had treatment or worked in a problem-solving group himself is not a "screwed-up" therapist, but is one who is protecting his patients from his own "hot potatoes."

72

Confrontation Versus Criticism

Confrontation is A-A with the implication that both are O.K. Criticism is P-C with the implication from the P that you are not O.K., and without my help you could not take care of yourself. I'm sure you've found that around some people you are suddenly spilling things, tripping over your own feet, using bad grammar, and becoming tongue-tied. These are people with whom you begin to feel not O.K. Once you're aware of this situation and if you keep subjecting yourself to it, that's up to you. But once you're aware that somebody's into saying subtly, "I'm O.K. and you're not," if you keep being with the person and feeling not O.K., you're collaborating. If the boss bawls you out and you agree to feel rotten, it's your decision to feel rotten. Words cannot hurt you. There are no bruises or broken bones. If you feel bad, it's you who are making yourself feel bad, because there is no feeling switch in your brain which someone else can turn on or off. If a patient says, "I just don't know what to do!" what he means is, "All you big strong Mommies and Daddies, tell me what to do." So the therapist or facilitator may say, "Which ego state are you in now?" or "You just turned on your helpless Child." This is a confrontation, Adult to Adult, and it means that you're O.K. Other confrontations: "Your right fist is clenched; you're shaking your head; you smiled when you said you were sad; your voice changed." Often the patient hears this as a put-down (P-C). "Your shoes are not shined, your slip is showing, you're late again," might be A-A or P-C depending on the tone of voice or situation. The following are more clearly P-C: What's wrong with you? You Shouldn't be late. You must finish your milk. Don't leave your clothes on the floor.

The Now

If the patient says she wants to get close to people, but she keeps her eyes on the floor and talks in a way so that no one can hear her, she is showing us in the room how she actually avoids people. She is saying both "Come here" and "Go away." So we talk to the patient about what she's doing right now. "You speak so quietly we can't hear, and you look at the floor." Patients might talk about what happened yesterday with their wives or husbands or bosses which avoids the people here in the room. No one knows for sure what happened yesterday, so we confront the patient about her behavior and feelings right here and now. If the patient says, "I'm angry," but she doesn't look angry, doesn't sound angry, and I say, "You don't look angry, you don't sound angry, you don't give clear messages." Or if the patient says, "I want something," with a hopeless, resigned look that says "I won't get it anyway, I'm already disappointed so don't even bother," we say, "You are asking in a way guaranteed not to get what you want." "What are you doing now?" "What are you feeling now?" "What do you want to do now?" are some questions the therapist asks to activate the patient's Adult in the service of her Child. If the patient says, "I never talk to anybody," I say, "Let's see you talk to somebody right now." And if she takes her gaze off the floor and looks into somebody's eyes, that's a big step. Another step is for the patient to maximize her choices. Patients often live, feel, and act as though they have no choices: "I have to do this terrible thing that I don't want to do." So it's a wow for the individual to discover that she has other choices. One way we do this is to change the phrase *I can't* to *I won't*. She Says, "I can't sew, I just can't sew a straight line," so we say, "You mean you *won't* sew a straight line." Or, "I can't get a job." "You mean you *won't* get a job." Or, "I can't stop drinking." "You mean you *won't* stop drinking." So we tell her in this way it's in her power to do it, if she wants to and is willing to do what it would take to change that situation. And then we ask her, "What other choices do you see for Sally?" So that the Adults in the group are useful to suggest alternatives. And usually the patient changes her tune from the helpless Child's "I have to" to the Adult's "I've decided to do X because it is the best of the alternatives." "I can't" is usually a rubberband for a person who, as a child, was required to do jobs too difficult for her, such as being asked, as a four-year-old, to mind a baby sister or, as a six-year-old to take care of her mother. "Now you're the man in the family (since your father is gone)."

Hook the Adult

The Child is good at playing games and having fun, but he is no good at solving problems. So he needs to turn on his Adult ego state when he's planning or problem solving. One way of doing this is to invite him to identify the ego state he has on. We sometimes use a tape recorder to play back his voice and then say, "Which ego state are you in? Who's talking now?" He needs his computing Adult to answer those questions. Another way to hook the Adult is for the therapist to confront patients about their vagueness. A lot of people get strokes for being vague. Clarify pronouns: What is *it*? Who is *he*? Clarify big words. We call attention to the patients' use of *you* instead of *I*. Or *we,* which is super Parent ("WE like to fold our clothes neatly, don't WE?") If you have a really wild Child in front of you, it's not easy to get the Adult back on. It is sometimes best to leave the patient for a few minutes until he cools down, and then you can come back to him. It is not always possible to hook the Adult. "What are you feeling now?" "I'm feeling sad." "Tell me about your sad feeling."

The therapist talks about cure. We will be partners with each other and with nature. We are not interested in making progress. ("Making progress" is a therapist's game). Some therapists give patients permission to scratch around and they say, "Well, we'll work on it," or they use words like "We'll sort it out." Or as somebody said after eight years of therapy, "Well, I still do what I always did, but now I know why." That's a therapist's game. And if the therapist has in his mind permission to cure the patient, it's a safeguard for the patient against archaeology (digging up old facts) or playing psychiatry (finding "interesting connections" between feelings, cataloguing them) and greenhouse (bringing this exotic feeling to the National Feeling Show). We're not interested in progress, we're interested in cure. If you do something bad, and you do it a tiny bit less next week, that's progress, but that isn't good TA. Let's say a patient drinks, and he drinks because he's not supposed to feel, and he's supposed to end up in the

74

gutter. So it isn't good enough if next week he gets drunk only four nights instead of five nights; that isn't a cure, that's "progress." What's O.K. is when he finds other ways to get exciting strokes and he lets himself feel. That's cure. Alcoholism is just a game which moves him along to the gutter where "I always knew I would end up." So we are not too pleased if he gets drunk three times or five times instead of six times. Or if you're onto script and you tell somebody, "Does it look like that's your script?" and they say, "Sort of" or "That's part of it," that means there's some part of them that still wants to keep the foot in the door about the old stuff. We smell a holdout and tell him he's hedging.

Another thing we've discovered: When a patient would come in with a big tragedy, we would become involved and give her lots of strokes for the tragedy and sadness, but if a person had a success, while we stroked her, we didn't stroke her as much as for a tragedy. We realized we were duplicating exactly the old pattern these people had going with their parents. So to give more strokes for feeling good than for tragedy, we have parties for successes in our group. Hardly a week goes by when we don't celebrate some happy success. We pass out champagne and snacks, and click glasses and toast our "making it" patient, quietly realizing in our heads that it's time to say good-by.

X. Getting to the Feelings and Other Short Stories

Lecture-Demonstration Therapy in a large group: Saturday, August 9, 1975, 4:00 to 5:00 p.m. at the International Transactional Analysis Association Summer Conference in San Francisco. The material below is an edited transcription of the tape recording. The room was hot and crowded. The participants had been at the conference all week, and we decided to enjoy the hour while teaching a few major concepts.

M = Morris   *N = Natalie*   *A = Audience*

N: Welcome!

A: Hi!

N: We had these neat exercises planned where we were all going to lie on floor. . .

A: Laughs. (There are 250 seats and 350 people. Every bit of floor space is filled. The exercise we had planned which involved lying on the floor and fantasizing childhood dreams was not possible because of the crowding.)

N: Can everybody see?

A: Yes.

M: (Takes the mike from Nat). We're glad to see everybody. What we're going to do today is talk about Feelings and Other Stories. And we're going to get to some feelings and we keep the stories short: one of the things we want to emphasize is that these two go together. We'll talk about a few of the guidelines that we use. Then we'll have some time for talking, doing things, or asking questions. So let's start.

      The first guideline: We speak clearly. That means if you don't understand me, either you clean out your ears or I talk more clearly. Speaking clearly means using language that an 8-year-old child can understand. Some of our students showed great improvement after they spoke louder and more clearly.

Another one of our guidelines is enjoying what we're doing and that's having fun and laughing. Another is that we don't work harder than the people we're working with. Because if we did, we wouldn't last very long.

We are aware of energy. The central theme in Transactional Analysis is the focus on *ACTION*. So in our lectures and marathons and groups, we encourage *action*. In our regular therapy groups, we encourage people to look at one another, to talk to one another, touch one another, wrestle, pull, push, hug, hold, massage, play footsy, hold hands.

We use TA theory.

A: What do you mean, you use TA theory?

M: Every person has a Parent ego state which nurtures, protects and gives rules for living, an Adult ego state which gets and gives information and solves problems, and a Child ego state which cries, plays, fights, asks for help, laughs. If a person is to change some undesired behavior (stealing, smoking, being depressed, over-working) he is more likely to make the change if all three ego states approve.

Another example of TA theory: People are more likely to be rigid and unchanged if they are stroke-deprived. They are more willing to change if they get lots of good strokes, which means lots of "I like you's. You are smart, sensitive helpful." Lots of hugs, touching, hand shaking, punching, pulling, screaming, laughing, crying. (A stroke is a sign of recognition: "Hello." It may be "I like you," or "I hate you." It may be a hug or a kick.)

The most common transaction in a TA group is Child to Parent. The client says, "I'm helpless, hurting, getting into trouble. What do I do?" The TA therapist uses his creativity at this point to say to the client, "I'm O.K. and you're O.K. What is your problem and how can you solve it?" thus crossing the transaction, changing the subject from "I'm so helpless" to "I have a problem which I can solve." The therapist does not say, "Oh, you poor, suffering, stupid, loveable jerk, can't you see that all you have to do is . . ." since that would be saying, "I'm O.K., you're not O.K." Any advice the therapist might give would be Parent to Child, and would assume "I'm O.K., you're not O.K." Actually a therapist has hundreds of possible interventions available when he hears a Child to Parent transaction, such as, "Would you diagram that transaction?" or "What do you experience now?" or "Your leg is twitching," or "Do an experiment" . . .

Another one of our guidelines is that even though we use TA theory, we avoid TA jargon. We want our students to understand what is going on rather than to use cliche words to flip through without understanding.

A: What do you mean?

N: When I hear something like, "Your Parent hooked my Child," I don't know what your Parent did and I don't know what my Child felt, and so if I want to know, I need to ask—and that slows down communication. If I say, "I want to get on with it," you don't know if that means I want to start getting hugs, or doing my homework, or looking for a husband, so the jargon gets between the experience and us. If we speak precisely, we are more likely to get what we want much faster. Sometimes when people come to visit us they say, "This is a TA group?. . . You don't use any TA words." Not only does using lots of TA jargon feel yucky to us, it seems very over-adapted to develop this private language that lots of people learn. Jargon may be very valuable for teaching, but not for therapy. So our groups sound different.

A: What do they sound like?

N: We talk *people talk*.

A: What's that?

M: We talk naturally. If I have a belly-ache, I say I have a belly-ache. I don't say "Your Parent hooked my driver." We have a patient who becomes furious when another patient acts helpless. He says, "I hate you when you act helpless!" instead of "Your Adapted Child hooked my Critical Parent." (Audience laughs)

Another guideline is that everybody gets strokes. They may get them whether they want them or not. So if they don't want them, they can say, "I don't want them." And that's something for us to watch. In a small group, usually 8 people, or in large groups, up to 150 people, we're watching to see who takes the strokes and who doesn't take the strokes. It's something for us to keep in mind. So we make sure that everybody gets offered strokes. There are several kinds of strokes which we use in groups: One is talking or listening. . . in other words, if you're listening to me and I need someone to listen, that's a stroke for me. If I talk to you and you need someone to talk to you, that's a stroke for you. Another good stroke is touching, or winking or looking.

We tell our students four rules about strokes. One is that there are plenty of strokes for everyone. We often act like there is a stroke short-age because there may have been a shortage of good strokes when we were children. But really, there are enough good strokes in this world for everyone. The second rule is that you are more likely to get what you want if you ask. A baby asks by crying. And if he wants a bottle, a pat on the head won't stop the crying. A healthy baby insists on getting fed when he wants it and a burp when he wants that. So ask for what you want. The third rule is that if you ask someone for a stroke, they may give it or may not. A mother busy on the telephone may not give her little girl a cookie. "No" doesn't mean "I don't love you" or "I will never give you a cookie again." "No" means "I don't want to give you a cookie right now." And the fourth rule is that if someone gives you a stroke and you don't want to accept it, you don't have to. Suppose someone you hate comes to give you a hug. You don't have to take the hug. Or suppose you are busy making out with your girlfriend after a long drought and someone comes and starts to give you some good advice on how to improve your posture... You don't have to take the advice.

N: Another thing we do is to keep moving. Rather than do a lengthy piece of work with one person in the group, we have a short series of transactions with someone and move on. If a person seems to get to something useful, we move on to somebody else. Some therapists stay as a leader of a group and do individual therapy in the group, doing a sizable and lengthy piece of work with somebody. There's sort of a chapter, and they talk back and forth 30 or 40 minutes and they finish it up, and then they go on to somebody else. We don't do that. We do a short thing, 5 to 10 minutes, and then we move on. The person is usually unfinished, and they usually come back and work some more...maybe a half hour later. What we notice is that in group treatment, frequently therapists and patients feel stuck with each other. Patients may work for a while in a group session, then not know how to get rid of the therapist when they feel they've had enough for the moment. They may have said something, and before they know it, they are stuck with each other and the therapist's thinking, "How the devil can I get away from this guy? I can't leave him when he's feeling so bad." And the patient's thinking, "Leave me alone! (Audience laughs) I'm sorry I opened my mouth."

M: I've got an idea about that. I was lying on the couch about 30 years ago, before most of you were born, and I was free-associating, day and night. Every once in a while, this guy—my analyst—would say something, like once a week. If he said three sentences in a row, I'd think, "Wow! What does that mean?" And I'd be thinking about the first sentence. Then he'd say something else and I wouldn't have digested the first one yet, and then he'd be saying even more. If he said three sentences in a row, I was lost. So, one thing I learned from my analyst: Say one thing *clearly* and then stop talking.

* * *

M: There are many concepts in TA which are useful, but we think the rubberband is one of the mose useful in the sense that it saves a lot of time. Is everybody familiar with rubberbands?

A: No. Yes. (Laughs) Who wrote it? (Laughs)

M: In TA, a rubberband is a snap-back to an old feeling. It's a feeling that somebody has, which is stronger than you would expect from the situation right now. And when I see it, I kind of smell it, I kind of feel it. When I'm doing therapy, I usually see 10 or 15 or 20 rubberbands in a two-hour session. And if I want to, I can work with any one of those, or ignore them or do something else. If you have this idea of rubberband feelings at your fingertips, or in your head, you can work with it. My favorite rubberband is one of the first ones I ever saw. A young man, about 19 years old, came into the group. There were six people present; he made seven. There were a couple of empty chairs. Two people were absent. And he said, "Where is everybody!" I started to say, "Mary said she was going to be late today, and John said he's away on vacation this week." And I'm thinking, "What the hell does he mean, 'Where's everybody?'—almost everybody's here." But I didn't say that. I said, "Hey, you see an empty chair and you're really feeling something. I bet when you were a little kid you saw an empty chair and it really meant something to you." And he said, "Yeah, when I was a little kid, when I was six years old, my father left, and every night my mother would set the table, and there would always be a place set for him, and his plate and his chair were always there, and he never came back." So, you can see what the rubberband is. An empty chair arouses much more energy and feeling in this man than in someone else. A feeling that has more energy, more intensity than you would expect can give you a clue, if you're alert, that the feeling happening now happened before.

I can think of another rubberband that was about chairs in a therapy session: this lady was doing a double-chair experiment, talking to a vacant chair. When I asked her to sit in it, she said, "Do I have to move? It's sort of a drag to sit in the other chair." I think to myself, "What's the big drag about getting up and moving to the other chair? So I said, "I bet when you were little they told you to be a good girl and sit in the chair." She said, "No, when I was a little girl, they tied me in the chair until I finished eating."

If you're alert to these little extra feelings, you can connect the intense feeling the person is putting on with an image of a child in a similar situation. Rubberbands help explain somebody's rather strong feeling, and by being aware of this, you can quickly get to the original sin, the original pain, the unfinished business.

A: Do you encourage rubberbands to help you find out...?

M: We don't encourage or discourage rubberbands. People are rubberbanding all over the place. I encourage myself to watch for them. People do what they do and then we see what they do. We train ourselves to imagine how they got that way.

N: We're all probably rubberbanding a good deal of the time. I bet you can take a minute and think about something this week to which you were aware you over-reacted. When it happens, you may even say to yourself, "What's the big deal? What am I feeling this bad for? or this sad for? or this scared for? What's this big feeling for this teeny incident from which there can probably be no dire consequences?" And I bet you can even think about and remember what you're rubberbanding to.

M: Some rubberbands feel good. When something like a perfume or the way the weather feels sets off nostalgia, that's a nice rubberband.

N: Another thing we do is use our feelings to facilitate group process. People in the group have a lot to give to one another...and a lot of the feedback and stroking and information our patients get, they get from one another. Sometimes somebody will be talking in a very boring way. I'll notice that I've withdrawn, tripped out, or am moving in and out, listening to a word or two and then thinking about what I'm going to be doing later, coming back and listening a little bit. It can be very helpful to ask the group, "How many people aren't paying attention?" Once in awhile I'm the only one with my hand up, but usually, many people raise their hands or say they're bored. The kids have left the room, gone away to some other places in their heads that are more interesting. The mommies hang around wanting to rescue the guy. Very often someone in the group says, "Yeah, I left you. I stopped listening to you a long time ago." The group often provides information like, "I really wouldn't take care of you for anything—you say you want to be taken care of, but most of us tuned you out, so I'm thinking you're angry or something like that and you want us to leave you." Sometimes the group will be able to pinpoint the exact spot in the person's story where everybody wandered away. Then I can ask him, "What were you feeling at this point?"

M: What most of this has to do with is our inside feelings. That is, we therapists use our inside feelings, our Child ego state, to help with the job when we're doing treatment. For example, suppose I'm in the group and I'm starting to get angry but I don't know why. I think, "Maybe I'm getting messages from somebody that he's angry but not showing it." So, I might say, "I'm getting angry. That's how I am now." Somebody might say, "Yeah, I wanted you to be angry," or "I'm angry with you." Or I might think, "I'm getting angry. Are others in the group angry too?" And, I might ask the group, "What are you feeling?" So we use our inside feelings to help us in the therapy to tell us where we are: "Hey, I'm getting a headache! I'm not supposed to get headaches...this is supposed to be fun, right?" So I will listen to my insides. I may or may not tell the group. I don't say every time I'm feeling something, because I would never stop talking.

N: Our methods have changed very much in the last year, and they'll probably be different a year from now. What Morrie's talking about is something we're doing lots more of this year than we did last year. We do a lot more work out of Child this year than we did last year. For example, if somebody is suffering and suffering, and I become aware that I feel like kicking him, I might use that information and say to the patient, "Usually when people feel real bad, I feel sympathetic, but when you keep suffering, I begin to feel angry with you...I'm starting to feel angry with you— I wish you'd quit suffering!" People are not quite so likely to feel hurt if I do that out of my Child. If I said that they were bad out of my Parent, they would probably feel real pain; but in talking out of my Child, I can take a lot of liberties which for some reason people feel less put down by and take as information. We joke. The group is often relaxed, friendly, joking.

Or if the patient says, "I can get lots of strokes here but I can't get them outside the group. The world outside is so different," we might respond out of Child a la Dick Tapley, "Why pay $25.00 a week for it here when you can get it outside free." Or out of Child to Miss Victim, "Poor little match girl!" or to the I'm-So-Great player, "Wow, folks! Superman is back!" With a patient who was making a contract to look at people who said, "I'll look at you when I talk to you," we replied, "Just say 'I'll look at you.'" And he said, "I'll look at you when I talk to you." We came back with: "Just say, 'I'll look at you, period. And if I talk to you, it's a bonus.'" We reduce the tortured heaviness so common in many groups by being aware of our own Child feelings. If I'm bored, I might say, "I'm bored," or might ask, "What are you all feeling?" If it's too heavy, I might ask everyone to "Stand up and get a hug, or let's all scream, 'It ain't fair!' or some other phrase which reflects the mood of the group.

Another point I want to make is that we do a lot more stroking than we do confronting. That is, if somebody starts to talk and they say, "I've been trying to get a job"—a lot of TA therapists hop on the patient because he or she said "try." So the patient says, "I'll try not to use 'try.' Ooops!" We'd be more likely to say, "Tell us some reasons you don't want a job," since "I'll try" often means "I won't." (Audience laughs) We don't think that people get to be O.K. just by learning a new set of rules or procedures. We think the only way you're going to enjoy your life is to know that you're O.K. now, however you talk and however your head is and however you're learning.

Energy is involved: If you're going to use an awful lot of energy checking yourself out, you're really not going to flow with yourself. And we like to flow with ourselves, and we'd like you to flow with *yourself*. Speak how you speak, and stand how you stand. We think it's neat for you the be the best kind of therapist you are, however you are and however you speak. And so, one of the things we do is stroke people when they do something that seems like it's good for them, rather than confronting them with things that we think are bad for them. One of our patients educated us to that. She said, "You know, in this group, if somebody has good luck, you say, 'Very nice, great!' and right away you move on to somebody else who's in agony." So we realized she was right, and we instituted a policy in our groups that if anybody achieves some success, or graduates from the group and says, "I'm O.K. Next week I'm leaving," then we have a party. In fact, at the drop of a hat we have a party. If we have gone a month without a party, something is wrong. When someone has a celebration, we stop the group, we bring out wine, or soda or something, and we toast the person: Like maybe they got married, or found a new job, or it's their birthday, or they graduated or learned to swim or enjoy bike-riding.

M: We discourage witch messages. We often hear therapists telling patients

"You have no intention of changing; you will never get well unless you..." "You just want to stay depressed; you don't want to get well..." "Have you ever thought of becoming psychotic? You will kill yourself some day unless you..." We understand how therapists may become discouraged. It ain't fair for them to pass on their despair to patients.

Are there any questions now, or requests?

A: I want to ask a question. How do you decide when something is dragging on, how do you decide when to switch it to something else? You said that you switched before the person's through.

M: Well, we would not switch if we thought the person was in really serious trouble. But unless we think someone's in danger of being left feeling suicidal or murderous, we would be willing to switch to someone else.

A.   You switch when you just feel like it?

N: We establish one thing and then get away to someone else. We want to avoid overload. For example, he has a big insight: "I can't study. Every time I start to study I start thinking about other things... My father said I was stupid. So I don't study to prove my father was right." Big insight. Great! We get away. Or he completes a contract. "I want to express my feelings." We ask him to tell people in the group what he feels about them. He does so. Or, a patient is agitated and confused. We ask her to close her eyes and get in touch with what she feels. She tells us about various sensations in her body and becomes more relaxed. She says, "I feel fine." We give her some strokes and go to someone else. And sometimes we get away when we get two or three "No's" in a row. We suggest something and the patient ignores us or says, "No." We could stop and confront: "We said so and so and you acted as if we hadn't said that. You didn't respond." ...or we could suggest something else, and the patient ignores again or says, "No." So we feel, "I'm O.K. and you're O.K." but right now we are not on the same wave length," so we get away and come back later. Sometimes we get away because the person's energy level has dropped and they control the group by doing nothing

M: Any more questions?

A: Keep telling more "how to's."

M: Okay. Well, we'll *do* some. We won't tell you, we'll *do* it. (Audience laughs) I'm sorry you're all feeling so good. (Audience laughs) 'Cause we're going to do something that would help you to feel better, but...

A: (Roars) Do it! Do it!

M: Okay. We'll do this exercise, and the way that we do it is you can just relax, close your eyes, and start breathing. (Audience laughs) But you gotta be *serious* about this.

A: (Laughs) Breathe in or breathe out?

M: The question was breathe in...repeat that. (Audience laughs) Get to your feeling, see what you're feeling. And when you exhale, make this little sound, like this, "Aaaahh..."

A: Aaaahh...

M: Aaaahh. And concentrate on what you're feeling.

A: (Laughs) Aaaahh's. (Laughs) Ah, ah, ah, (Laughs) (Audience is laughing for a full minute.)

N: Something's going wrong.

A: (Roars, laughs, shouts) Something is going *right!*

M: What I want to do...see what you're feeling in your head, what you're feeling in your neck, what you're feeling in your chest, or back or hips or legs or behind, or whatever. Feel your body. Pay attention to it. Your body is real precious, that's your Child. See what's going on with your Child. Some places may hurt, and some places may feel sad, and some place you may feel happy, and some place you may feel angry or disappointed or irritated or scared or whatever. Get in touch with your feelings...and continue to breathe deeply. Breathing deeply will give you energy and may help you with your feeling, which may get bigger or may get smaller. Breathe deeply.... (Pause for 30 seconds while audience sits with eyes closed and very quiet) And this feeling that you have is real precious, so don't get away from it. Keep it. Hold it. See what it is. You've been at a big conference for several days, seen a lot of people, gotten a lot of strokes. Sometimes this leaves you feeling real good, sometimes it gives you a pain...someplace. So get in touch with that. Everybody got it? Would you open your eyes and look around and talk to your neighbor about what you found out, just for a minute; then your neighbor will tell you what he or she found out.

A: (Talking for 2 minutes. Some people can be heard to say they feel real sad; others say they feel good. Nearly everyone is talking or listening to someone.)

M: Would everybody...we're going to do a little research, and it will take about one or two minutes. You know, lots of times research takes five years, a million dollars, and we do this research over and over again to keep testing it out. Give yourself a number, on a scale zero to 100. Zero means you're feeling awful; 100 means you're feeling ecstatic; 50, you're in between. Don't tell anybody your number; just think about what number you have. Give yourself a number zero to 100—zero's awful, 100's wonderful, 75 is real good, 25 is low. Everybody got their number? Now stand up. (Everyone stands) *Now* give yourself a number. You may have the same number, you may have a different number. Everybody got a number? How many felt better when you stood up? Raise your hands! (About 200 raised their hands) How many got worse when you stood up? Raise your hands. (About 10 people)

A: Can we yell our numbers?

M: No. (Audience laughs) How many stayed the same? (About 50 people) Okay, most people felt better after they stood up, so one way to help most people feel better, just tell them to stand up. (Audience laughs) Everybody keep standing and everybody turn to your right (Audience turns) Rub the person's back in front of you. (Audience does this)

A: (Sounds of agreement and delight for 40 seconds)

M: That's enough, that's enough.

A: No! No!

M: Turn around and rub the back of the other . . . (Audience does this)

A: More ahhh's (1 minute).

M: That's enough.

A: Settles down (Takes about 30 seconds).

M: Now how many people felt better when they got rubbed on the back?

A: (Most people raise their hands and shout or applaud)

M: How many felt worse? One? (One)

A: Can we do it again? (Laughs)

M: How many felt the same? One? One person felt the same, and one person felt worse, and 300 people felt better. Here's a kind of research project that can be tested out. We need a whole lot more research to see which methods work best.

                               *   *   *

M: If we expect people to change their behavior, we believe they are more likely to make small changes before large ones. To buy a house or car he must first save a few dollars a month. To learn to swim he must first go into the water. To dance he must first move to the music. To ask for strokes directly he must first look at someone. To get to explosive feelings it is helpful for the patient first to breathe deeply, then to stand up, then to look at people, then make a noise on the exhale, then stick out his tongue, then to shout at each other, and finally push each other, shouting.

     We recall Fritz Perls working with a person having a recurring dream. In the dream the lady was entering a room. As she acted out entering, she said, "I'm afraid to go in." Fritz said, "Open the door." She said, "I'm scared." Fritz said, "Open the door just a little bit." And she did. And the therapy continued. When we see a person wanting to do something he won't do at this moment, it is helpful to take a small step first. If he is unwilling to leave the house, he can imagine walking out the door, walking to the street, 15 feet, and returning to the house. If he won't get a job, we ask him to: (1) Tell how good it is not to work; (2) Describe unpleasant work situations in his past; (3) Describe pleasant work situations in his past; (4) Describe his early decision not to grow up or work, and make a new decision; and (5) To get a job 1 hour a week.

* * *

We have given you a brief overview of some of our current therapeutic prejudices. We are not satisfied that our therapy is as effective as it could be. Ideally, therapy would mean a 10 or 15 minute interview which would change the person's life. Occasionally (not often enough) we have had that experience. Meanwhile, we provide an environment rich in fun, pleasure, pain and information while we watch the participants in our groups change their behavior over a period of months or one, two or three years. One of the most delicate problems is how to show we care about someone without getting into a rescue, i.e. without getting too actively involved in "saving" them, thinking for them, or advising them. All of these would rip-off the patient's initiative. We make a point never to be more active than the patient, and never to work harder than he does. We need better methods of therapy. In our TA groups we see 100 to 200 persons per week, of whom a high percentage get well. Better methods of therapy would mean a higher percentage would get well faster, and that's what we are looking for.

XI. Exercises

Here are some five-to-thirty-minute exercises we have used in classes and workshops to illustrate concepts, expand awareness, develop assertiveness, warm up a cold place, free up rigidities. Some of the exercises were performed or suggested by others, in which cases their names appear. We don't know the source of many.

In all exercises, if some people don't want to participate, we don't force or push them, but ask them what they felt about doing or not doing the exercise. The optimum length of time for an exercise is judged by the leader. We usually stop an exercise when interest is still high, before energy lags.

1. The Social Values. Close your eyes and think of what you want out of life. (2 minutes) Now open your eyes and get a partner, and partners tell each other what they want. (2 minutes) Leader writes list on chalk board.

2. My Best Learning Experience. Everyone writes down his or her best learning experience, and then the worst. Talk to your partner about this. Partners then tell the entire group.

3. What I Like About Children. Partners tell each other "what I like about children" and "what I dislike."

4. Friends. Close your eyes and think of a friend you used to have but have no more. What made this person a friend? How did you separate? (3 minutes) Open your eyes and tell your partner.

5. My Physical Sensations. Tell your partner just what you are experiencing now. Tell him the minor sensations you feel—your heart beating, itching, pressures, air in nostrils or mouth, your tongue feeling your teeth, stomach sensations, slight or strong pains. (3 or 4 minutes each) Now tell your partner how these sensations change as you describe them.

6. Changing the World. In small groups, discuss changes you would like to see in the world. (5 minutes) Now talk about what you sense in your body. What happens in your body when you talk about changing your world?

7. It Ain't Fair. Talk to your group about what you think is not fair. (5 minutes) Now talk about what you can do to change what is not fair.

8. Whom I Like to Listen to Me. Talk with your partner about whom you like to talk to, whom you like to listen to you. See if you can understand what is special about that person or group that listens to you.

9. My Symptoms. (Irma Lee Shepard) Close your eyes. Think of a pain you have had in the past few months. Imagine it is much worse. How is your life different? Now talk to your pain. What does the pain say back to you? Open your eyes and tell the group what your pain said. Repeat what it said to several persons. Now— whom would you like to say that to? (What the pain said to us is often what we would like to say to someone else.)

10. My Best Teacher. Think of the best teacher you ever had. How was this teacher different? Talk to your partner about what you learned.

11. I Won't Ask. Close your eyes and think of times you wanted to say something or ask for something and did not do it. (1 minute) Now think of times when you were a child and you wanted something and asked for it and got into trouble asking, or were disappointed. See if you can relate your childhood experiences of asking with your decisions not to ask now.

12. Lick Me (A Wrestling Exercise). (The daughters of Nancy Radeloff) Pick a partner. Tell your partner one spot on your body that you must not lick. For example, your elbow or nose or back of neck. Your partner tries to lick that part and you prevent him from doing that. A variation of this is to tell your partner one spot on your body that she must not touch and then her part of the game is to touch that spot. This is best done in a room with plenty of space and mats or thick rugs on the floor.

13. What Do You Want to Learn? Close your eyes. Think of 2 or 3 things you would like to learn. (3 minutes) Open your eyes. Write down what you would like to learn. (3 minutes) Form groups of 4 persons and tell each other what you wrote. (10 minutes) Teacher then asks each person to tell what he would like to learn, and if possible helps make arrangements for student to learn that in the classroom at this session.

14. My Parents' Travels. Close your eyes and think of your parents moving from job to job or from house to house. How have these moves affected your life? Talk to your partner about what you found out.

15. Early Strokes. Close your eyes. Think of yourself as very little. What are the earliest good or bad strokes that you got? What did you do? What did the person say or do to you? How is that like your life today?

16. Whom Would You Most Like to Invite? Form into groups with 5 or 6 persons in a group. Each person writes down the names of any 6 persons living or dead whom you would like to be guests at a party and give one reason for inviting each. Don't tell anyone whom you are inviting, and don't put your own name on your slip of paper. Collect the lists and pass them around to others in the group so that each group member has someone else's list, and reads the names of the guests out loud. Others in the group guess who wrote each list.

17. Sentence Completions. (Nat Brandon) There are hundreds of possible sentences, and ways of doing this. If the group is fewer than 9 persons, they may stand in a circle while one member walks around inside the circle and completes the sentences. If the group is around 15, two circles may be formed. If the group is over 20, persons may stand facing each other in pairs while the teacher reads off the sentences and each partner says the sentences and completions to each other. Here are a few suggested sentence completions:

> Five things I like about myself are...
> Five things I don't like about myself are...
> Ever since I was a child...
> My mother was usually...
> Mother never...
> Father...
> I was ashamed when...
> One of the things I'm really angry about is...

18. Draw a Picture to Music. Play some mood music. Ask the group to paint or draw a picture that tells a story about the music. If you have no paints, you can say "Close your eyes. Listen to the music. Make up a story about it. Open your eyes and write down the story. Read it to your partner."

19. Be Little and Paint. Close your eyes. Imagine you are three or four years old. Feel how helpless you are, your lonely feelings, your fears, your happy feelings. Draw a picture or paint as you would if you were three or four. Talk to your group as you do this.

20. Caring for Baby. (Dixie Robinson) Get a partner. One is a six-week-old baby and one is Mama or Daddy. Baby is lying down asleep. (Babies lie down and close their eyes.) Baby starts to cry—it's time for a bottle. Leader writes on board: "Take care of baby," and parents do so. Baby cries again—has a wet diaper. Leader writes on board: "Don't do anything." (wait 3 minutes) Discuss what happened.

21. Baby Is 9 Months Old. (Dixie Robinson) Get a partner. One is parent and one is 9 months old and is able to crawl. Leader writes on board: "Keep baby quiet and in one place." (5 minutes) Leader writes on board: "Let baby crawl around." (5 minutes) Discuss what you experienced.

22. Asking for What You Want. Close your eyes and think of things you wanted, people you wanted to do something for you, you said *yes* when you wanted to say *no,* when you did not ask for what you want, or you asked in a way guaranteed not to get what you want. (3 minutes) Now think back to when you were little and you wanted things and did not ask. (3 minutes) Talk to your partner about your memories.

23. Your Ma Talks About You to a Friend. A. Get a partner. Be your mother talking about you to a friend when you are 5 to 10 years old. (After 5 to 10 minutes partners switch so that both have a chance to be mother talking about them. B. Be your mother talking about you to a friend today. (5 to 10 minutes) How is what she says today the same and different from when you were little? (5 to 10 minutes)

24. Waiting...While the World Goes By. A lot of people are waiting. When something goes wrong, they wait for it to get better. Johnny wanted a bike and he got a job in a grocery store to make the money to buy a bike. His brother Gene stayed home and waited while his brother had fun riding his bike. When do you play the waiting game? What do you want that you are not getting, and that you are waiting for?

25. Masks. Close your eyes and think of how you show or don't show what you really feel. Or say or don't say what you really think. Which of these masks do you wear?

Happy face	Dead pan
Sad sack	I've got a secret
I don't have fun, so you shouldn't	You're O.K. and I'm not
I'm available	Show me yours and I'll comment on it
I'm shy	Spaced out—like a kid with a load in his pants
I'm pissed off, angry	
I'm sicky icky	The silent sufferer
I'll do anything to please you	Tragic queen
Let's complain	Listen to how great I am
Just listen, you don't have to say a word	Talk to me, I'll listen to you

26. Show and Tell. Each person with news in the group tells the news event about himself. Today was my birthday, I got a job, I had my first date, I got fired, I started a new project. . . .

27. My Ancestry. Think of your parents and other ancestors. What was their race, nationality, religious backgrounds? Were they rich, poor, middle class? How have these factors influenced what you do, what you believe, how you live, and how you feel about yourself and others.

28. Teaching-Learning Network. (Eliezer Krumbein) Each person writes down two or three things he would like to learn. A list of who wants to learn what is posted on the bulletin board thus:

Name	Wants to Learn	Wants to Teach
Sam	to repair a faucet	how to ride a bike

Teachers and learners get together at their own time and place.

29. Chin In, Chin out, Chin up. (Myrna Haimowitz) Stand with your eyes closed. Experience your posture. Put your hand on the back of your neck as you move your chin way out in front and then move your chin down on your chest, and then your chin up in the air. Do this slowly and notice how this affects your breathing, affects your spine. Open your eyes and put your hand on the back of your partner's neck as partner moves chin out, in and up. Switch. Talk to your partner about what you observed.

30. My Body, My Shame. In groups of from 2 to 6, imagine you are naked right now. What parts of your body would you be ashamed of. Talk to the group.

31. I See, I Imagine. Close your eyes and let your eyes see whatever they will see. Imagine whatever you imagine (4 minutes). In groups of 2, tell what you did.

32. Our Group. In groups of 5 or 6, members of the group tell each other what they like and don't like about each other. The group moves to another part of the room and tell their experiences about how it was to move. Members of the group stand facing each other, holding hands and pushing against each other in pairs, growling, roaring and shoving, and talk about what they experienced. Or they Indian wrestle, standing or lying on the floor. Members talk about their thoughts and feelings after the exercise.

33. I Owe You and You Owe Me. (June Shane) Discuss with your small group what you owe people, and how that controls what you do or avoid doing; and what they owe you and how that controls their behavior towards you and others. How do their expectations stop you from doing certain things and how do your expectations get them to do or to stop doing certain things?

34. Energy Building. Stand up, standing arm's length apart. Bend over, hands and head falling down loose as far as possible, exhaling as you bend. Now raise your hands slowly, inhaling until your hands are raised above your head. Hold them there for a moment and then slowly exhale and bend to the floor. (10 times)

35. My Joys. (a) Discuss with a partner your joys at home: food, peace, excitement, rest, other. (5 minutes) (b) Change partners. Discuss with your partner your joys at work, excitement, challenge, frustrations, accomplishments. (5 minutes) (c) Change partners. Discuss with your partner your joys at school (5 minutes)

(d) Change partners. Discuss with your partner your joys in your free time. (5 minutes).

Increasing Your Joys. (e) Change partners. Discuss with your partner how you might increase your joys at work (like talking to fellow workers, taking breaks, staying in the now, day-dreaming, bringing fun foods, other). (5 minutes) (f) Change partners. Discuss with your partner how you might enjoy your home life more (like play games, talk, watch TV, fight, make love, other). (5 minutes) (g) Change partners. Discuss how you might·enjoy your free time more. (5 minutes)

36. Look at a Small Object and Breathe Your Name. Sit up straight and comfortably, chin down, head up. Select a small object or mark across the room to look at. See only the object. Let your eyes blink naturally. Breathe in, and when you exhale, whisper your name, or the name of someone you love. (5 minutes)

37. Problems I Need to Solve. (a) Select a partner. Discuss "times when I don't think or speak as well as I might." (5 minutes) (b) Change partners. Discuss "times when I don't feel as good as I might." (5 minutes) (c) Change partners. Discuss "times when I don't do what I would like." (5 minutes) (d) Change partners. Discuss "my resentments." (5 minutes) (d) Change partners. Discuss "my fears." (5 minutes) (f) Change partners. Discuss "my sadness." (5 minutes) (g) Change partners. Discuss "my hopes." (5 minutes) (h) Change partners. Discuss "my creativity" (5 minutes) (i) Change partners. Discuss "my problems I need to solve." (5 minutes)

38. Walk to Music. If people are in all-day programs, a good 10-minute break is to walk to music, with focus on breathing. On the exhale say, "I am walking and dancing; and we are all part of the universe."

39. I Like You, Nose. Sit or lie down in a comfortable position, close your eyes, and touch your nose and say, "I like you nose." Let your hand touch your forehead, your eyes, your mouth, and tell each part, "I like you because...." Then let your hand touch each part of your body and say something nice to it.

40. Giving People or Things Up, Letting Go. Discuss with your partner how you let go of people, old clothes, old furniture, books, toys, your baby blanket, old fears, old dreams, old resentments. Do you ever dream of going off in a car and leaving everything?

41. People Above Me and Below Me. Discuss with your partner how you decide that people are above you or below you, and how you therefore respond to them, have certain expectations of them, because you have placed them in a superior or inferior position or role.

42. My Defiance. Discuss with your small group, "my defiance," how I refuse to give in to some people or ideas, refuse to listen to some people or ideas, refuse to look at some people.

43. My Childhood Fantasy. Close your eyes and think about something you used to think about as a child...a childhood fantasy. Do you still think about it? What did this fantasy mean to you as a child?

44. My Favorite Sexual Fantasy. Close your eyes and think of your various sexual fantasies. Pick three which are most frequent for you. Now pick one which you could call your favorite. Now look at yourself. Are you friendly or angry? Are you active or passive? Are you the chaser or are you being chased? Do you hold out or are you easy to get? What is your feeling in this fantasy? Pleasure, pain, scared, sad? Open your eyes and tell your partner.

45. My Favorite Bible Story. Think of two or three Bible stories you know. Tell yourself the stories briefly. Which one stands out as your favorite? How is that story like your life today?

46. I'm for Sale. Write an advertisement for the want ads saying "I'm for sale." Take three minutes to write this out. Now read your ads in small groups.

47. Being Two. (Group House) The two-year-old child is establishing himself as a separate person. He may say, "I want some candy," and when you give it to him, he says, "I don't want it." He is saying, "I can think for myself," and he does this by being contrary. He wants some ice cream, and when his mother says, "Here is some ice cream," he says, "I don't want it." His most common word is "NO." Now close your eyes and think how you are still two, how there is a two-year-old inside you who still says "No" even when he wants to say "Yes."

48. Being Three. The three-year-old child is interested in the world. He asks lots of questions. "Why does it rain?" He asks different people for permission: "Hey, Mom, can I go out?" Mom says, "Yes." He asks Dad, "Can I go out?" Dad says "No." So he gets Mom and Dad to fight. His parents in his head are fighting. One says "You should be nice;" the other says, "You should stand up for your rights." There is some belief that parents get divorced when the child is three because the three-year-old got them to fight. When the child becomes separate from his mother, his father becomes very important, so he has to check things out with father. A man calls some friends for dinner and says, "Pot luck." He calls others, and says he is bringing the food, and it's at someone else's house, so there is a big mix-up and lots of phone calls to get it straight. How are you like a three-year-old? When do you do some of these kinds of things?

49. Being Four. With some four-year-olds, when you say, "How are you?" they say "What do *you* care?" They turn love to hate. They have to think about everything. Nothing comes easy, nothing comes automatically, they get tired and slip into thoughts about witches and monsters. They control themselves by scaring (you and them). Talking is a way of controlling the energy. When they get tired, they regress to age three and start asking a lot of questions as a three-year-old does, not because they want information, but because they already know the answer to most of their questions, so it must be for some other purpose. If you know any four-year-olds, check it out and see if they have these qualities, or whether they would best be described in other ways. When are you like a four-year-old?

50. Solving Problems. People can solve problems; they know what they need, and often they need parenting. If the problem is to get parenting, then they will do what they need to get parenting: come late, spill coffee, get into fights, play stupid, ask questions, or other troubles, so that the parents around get angry at them. That is what they need: to get parents angry at them. How do you get parents angry at you? What other kinds of parenting is it possible for you to get? Talk in groups of three about this.

51. Being Thirteen. A 13-year-old sometimes acts like a one-year-old. A girl who had been making her own sandwiches starts asking Ma to make them for her. She needs her new parts validated. She goes back to being oral. She needs to know it's O.K. to grow and have hair and breasts. One woman in the group was 45 and flat chested and she wanted someone to stroke her breasts so they would get larger. As if you let boys stroke them, they get larger. People need their new parts validated (stroked) just like as a baby they need all parts stroked. How do you sometimes go back to being a one-year-old? Which of your parts do you want stroked.

52. The Newborn Baby. The newborn baby needs strokes, needs food, and it cries automatically when in discomfort. It does not cry to make Mom mad. Babies cannot think at birth; they can only feel. Mothers and fathers can think and act. When a baby hurts, it hurts all over, the whole world hurts. I can't exist unless someone does something for me. All I can do is cry. When grown-up people feel like this, they feel like the newborn who is really helpless. A baby is adequate if it can cry. It is not demeaning for a baby to cry, but if a baby does not get what it needs, it feels inadequate: "If I ask for what I need, I won't get it, and something worse will happen." This was a thought of a woman whose mother spanked her when she fell down the stairs and cried. When do you feel like a newborn? What do you do to think and act so that you won't feel helpless?

53. Teenagers. The 14-year-old may be like a two-year-old; and the 15-year-old like a 3 and a 16-year-old like a 4, but the 17 year old is like the 5-year-old, who is getting ready to leave the family. At age 5 or 6 the child goes off from the family to school. They need to know they can leave and someone cares for them. They may be afraid of something terrible if they leave, perhaps that the family will be

94

destroyed. Everyone feels like leaving their family from time to time. When do you feel like leaving? What terrible thoughts stop you? How could you make your life in your family better?

54. Feeling Left Out. Imagine a scene in which two or three people are talking or arguing and you are standing there, feeling not in, feeling left out. Now think back to when you were a child, and you saw your parents talking or arguing and you felt left out. What would you like to say to them?

55. Then and Now. (Liz Schoeneberger) Partners say to each other: As a child I pleased my (mother, father, grandparent, brother, sister, etc.) when I.... Close your eyes and review the statements you made. Open your eyes and tell your partner "how I continue this same behavior now. Is it what I want to do?"

56. My Secret Parent. (Liz) Partners to each other: (a) Children please me when they.... (b) Children displease me when they.... Discuss what you find out about your Parent from this exercise. What messages do you give your Child from your Parent? Did you discover any secret Parent messages?

57. If I Were Young Again. (Liz) In groups of 5 or 6 seated in a circle, each member says, "If I were young again, I would want..." (fill in what you would want). Now think of ways to get from the group members what you said you would want.

58. In Order to Survive. (Liz) Think of yourself as very young and say to yourself, "In order to survive, I need my mother's love and protection. To get this love and protection I must be...." (List all the Be's that come into your head.) Then, change it, "To get this love and protection I must *not*...."

59. My Favorite TV Character. (Liz) Write down your favorite TV person or fairy tale or historic person. Describe the dress, behavior, phrases that describe the person. In groups of 3 or 4 be the person you described, tell about yourself, how you are dressed, what you do. Which of the 4 positions is this person in most of the time (I'm O.K. etc.) How are you like this person?

60. Footsie. Sit in a circle, remove shoes and socks, and move in close enough so that feet touch center of circle. Cover feet with a sheet or blanket, and rub feet. Talk about your experiences.

61. Slap Hands. Stand in pairs. Slap each others' hands. Shout, "Me! You!" to show each is a different person.

62. Be Scared. To get in touch with fear, individuals or groups sit, hands in lap, shoulders scrunched up, head down, and shake, take big breath and hold it. Usually fear is dissipated by deep breathing.

63. Interlocking Rackets. For more advanced students. Students identify their rackets and describe how their racket interlocks with their parents, spouse or patients. For example:

I'm disappointed. I'm a disappointment.

Mother was expecting to be gypped, deprived, and whatever I did was disappointing. Sometimes "I'm disappointed" comes from having been born the wrong sex. Ma had 5 boys and then I came along, another boy. She wanted me to be a girl. No matter what I did she was disappointed, and now, no matter what I do, I'm disappointed.

Another common example:

Patient plays stupid, confused, has a poor little me racket. Therapist has a rescuer, smart-ass racket, plays hard to clarify patient's muddled statements.

64. I Waited for You: So You Wait for Me. How do you feel about waiting for people who come late? Think of the last couple of times that happened. Now think of times when you were a child and had to wait for your parents while they talked to people, how you waited in school, stood in line at the cafeteria or to get into the theatre. How do you keep people waiting for you now? Or, how do people keep you waiting?

65. Being Soft. Paintings by Dali show watches looking soft, melting, and he describes time as soft, tender, loving. Think of times when you felt soft and tender, when you melted. . . . Now, think of times when you were hard. . . . What do you do when you are soft? . . . And, what do you do when you are hard?

66. Writing on the Wall. Close your eyes and imagine you are in a familiar room and you see writing on the wall. You read it. . . . Open your eyes.

67. How I Used to Get Strokes. Close your eyes. Think of ways you used to get strokes. Take a minute or two. Open your eyes. Now tell your partner what you found out.

68. The Smoking Game: P A C for Smokers. Here are some P A C messages about smoking. Close your eyes while I read them to you:

P Smoking is not clean; it's O.K. to kill yourself; it's a filthy habit.

A It's something to do; it may cause cancer, emphysema or heart failure; It costs money.

C It keeps my hands away from my genitals; it burns my eyes and throat; I can blow it in your face.

Now think about these messages. Which ones do you hear the loudest? Are there other messages you have? Open your eyes and talk to your group about this.

69. Ten Big Breaths and a Pillow. Everyone sit up straight and hold your pillow in your lap. Take ten very big breaths making a loud sound on the inhale and also on the exhale. All together—one—two—slowly and big—three—four—make a big sound on the inhale and on the exhale—five—six—seven—eight—nine—ten. Now do to the pillow whatever feelings you have: hug it, twist it, pound it, talk to it. If you are angry, be angry—be very angry. If you are sad, be very sad. If you are happy, be happy. If you are scared, say so.

70. Feeling, Thinking and Acting = C A P. We have a Child that feels, the an Adult who says, "Oh! I see that you feel (hungry—sad—tired, etc.)," and a Parent who says, "If you feel hungry, I'll get you some food; and if you are tired, I'll hold you or let you sleep." When all three parts are in good working condition, the Child feels, the Adult thinks about this, and the Parent takes action to help the Child. Close your eyes and think about an important feeling you have been having in the last ten minutes, or anytime today. What did you think about that feeling? And what action did you take or not take? Think about this for 2 minutes. Open your eyes and talk to your partner about what you learned.

71. Out of the Dark Cave. Close your eyes. You are standing in a forest behind a tree. It is dark and you are looking ahead of you around the tree. You see a cave, and as you look, you see something move inside the cave. You see something come out of the cave. Open your eyes and tell your partner what you saw. Take two minutes. After two minutes, ask the class, "What did you see? How did you feel?"

72. A Little Child. Close your eyes and imagine you are a child. What is your position and feelings as you imagine it. Where are you in your family? Open your eyes and tell your partner.

73. A Free Week-End. It's Friday night and you have nothing to do over the week-end. You can do almost anything you like. Think of two or three things you would like to do, but something stops you. Think of how you can do what you want. Now talk to your group about what you learned.

74. A Sign on the Gate. Close your eyes. Imagine you are in a forest. There is a path. You walk down the path which is narrow and has trees on both sides. You see a fence and walk up to the gate. There is a sign on the gate. You read the sign. What do you feel? Open your eyes. What did the sign say?

75. The Child and the Adult. Close your eyes and think of something you want that you are not getting. Call this problem ABC. Who is involved with you in this problem? Whom are you blaming? Who is O.K. and who is not O.K.? What are you saying to yourself? If you are blaming yourself or someone else, this is probably your Child ego state. Now think of the problem this way: I want ABC and what is necessary for me to get ABC? What are the circumstances, what are the actions needed. To get ABC I must XYZ. This is probably your Adult. Open your eyes and share what you learned with your group.

76. A Holiday Memory. (Ted Novey) *To be used at some holiday time.* We are celebrating _____ holiday this week. Think back to when you were younger and remember something important to you that happened on this holiday. Tell your partner.

77. What I Learned to Feel. (Jon Wagner) Indicate be quiet for 1 or 2 minutes. Lie on the floor. Close your eyes and think of your mother when you were small. Think of her being happy. What was she doing? Were you happy when she was happy? (Say nothing for one minute.) Think of your mother being sad. When was she sad? How did you feel when she wàs sad? How did you know she was sad? . . . Think of her being afraid. How could you tell she was afraid? . . . Did you tell her when you were afraid? . . . When was she angry? When she was angry with someone, did you side with her or with the other person? . . . Now think of your father. When was he sad? (Go through the other feelings for father: scared, happy, angry.) . . . What have you learned about your own feelings? . . . Now open your eyes. . . look around. . . tell your partner what you learned.

78. Stroking. (Ruth McClendon) Class sits in groups of 4 or 5. Whoever is "It" is given strokes by all others in the group. "It" does not say "Thank you" but enjoys the strokes. Then "It" asks each group member for special strokes that "It" wants, such as compliments, massage, hugs, to be held and rocked, etc. unconditionally accepting all the good strokes without returning words in exchange for the strokes.

79. Dinner Time. Close your eyes and remember dinner time when you were younger. Who talked? Did they tell you to eat, to eat less, to eat more, to hurry, to slow down? How did you get strokes at dinner time? What was happy or painful? How are you still doing the same things?

80. My First Day in School. Think of your first day in school. How did you get to school? What happened that you remember about getting to school and getting home? What happened in school or on the school grounds? What did you do on that first day that you are still doing?

81. Talk to Your Image. (John Stevens) Close your eyes and take three deep breaths, and as you exhale, let all the tensions leave your body, and become more and more relaxed. Now see yourself in a large mirror and talk to your image. What do you like? What should be changed? Look at your body, your clothes, posture. Look at the image and study it and see what you are concerned about. Tell the image, "I am concerned about. . . ." Now be the image and reply. How do you feel? How do your answer yourself—in a friendly way, harshly?

82. Talk to Your Father. Close your eyes and talk to your father. Tell him, "I have always wanted you to like me," and be your father answering. Continue the conversation, being yourself and then being your father. What did you find out?

83. Where Do You Get Your Strokes? (Ted Wilt) Make a list of where you get your strokes (friends, relatives, dog, library, supermarket, tennis court, etc.) Give a relative percentage to each, showing which are most numerous, for example, 30% from children, 10% from the dog, etc. Now close your eyes and figure out how your stroking patterns affect what you do—how you structure your time.

84. If I Were Intimate With You... (Charles Kelley) Group stands in a circle, facing inside the circle, counting off in two's (one, two, one, two, etc.). Everyone turns to the right. All persons who are No. 1 turn around and face your partner. Everyone facing clockwise, say to your partner, "When I look at you, I feel...." Finish the sentence and repeat for 3 minutes, "When I look at you I feel...." Now, No. 1's move forward and get a new partner. Say, "One thing I like about you is...." and repeat for three minutes. Ditto. And then, "One thing I don't like about you is...." and "If I were intimate with you I would...."

85. My Doll Was Thrown Away. (Frances Winston) Close your eyes and remember when something you owned was thrown away by your parents or someone, how you felt and what you thought about it. Did you do anything about it? Talk to your partner about this.

86. How People Get Fired. Close your eyes and think of two or three people where you work who got fired, or two or three people you know who got fired. What happened that they were fired? What would have to happen for you to get fired? Talk to your group about this.

87. You Will Die. There is a chance you will die in one of 4 or 5 ways. Which one is most likely for you? Now imagine that at 11 P.M. tonight you will die in that way. What will you do between now and then?

88. Unfinished Business. (Charles Kelley) Group divides into pairs. Worker lies on mat, partner sits near worker, watching worker to be sure he is safe during the discharge. Worker on mat breathes very deeply, exhaling with a sound, knees raised, mouth open, eyes open, for 10 or 15 minutes. (If worker's fingers begin to curl or get stiff, ask worker to take a breath and hold it for one minute and then to breathe in shallow breaths, and stop the exercise because the deep breathing is causing loss of carbonic acid, blood level is losing acidity and body metabolism is changed.) Tell workers after 10 or 15 minutes of deep breathing to talk to someone they have unfinished business with, someone they are angry with or afraid of or sad about. Suggest statements like, "Get off my back!" or "What I'm angry about is..." or "I need you—help me" or "Leave me alone!" Partner sits quietly, his purpose is to be sure worker is safe and knows someone is with him.

89. A Secret. Think of a secret you have, that you don't tell anyone. . . . Now, imagine you tell someone your secret. . .

90. Bragging. Everyone think of something you would like to brag about. . . . Who wants to walk around and brag? A few people take turns.

91. Orchestral Breathing. (Myrna Halmowitz) Group stands in circle. Leader says, "When I raise my hands, inhale. If I raise high, take a big breath and hold it until I lower my hands. If I raise my hands a little, take a little breath." Leader raises hands, sometimes high, sometimes a little, sometimes fast, sometimes slow.

92. Anywhere You Want. Close your eyes and imagine you see a map of the earth spread out. You look and see the seven seas and all the continents. If you could be anywhere you want, where would you be? Who would be with you? What keeps you from being there? What do you need to do to get there?

93. Scared for Whom? If a little kid starts to run out in the street, his parents get scared. So, if he is taught to be scared to run out in the street, then his parents don't have to be scared any more. Think of who felt like a big shot when you were scared as a child. Who comforted you, or told you "Don't be a sissy" or "Don't be a scaredy cat?" Think of what scared you as a child and what you did when you were scared. Did you tell anyone?

94. My Grandmother. Close your eyes and remember your grandmother (or both of them). What special things did she do for you? What restrictions did she place on you? How was your life different because of her? What did you have to do for her? What did you feel when she died? What did you tell yourself? If she is still alive, what do you want to tell her before she dies?

95. My Martyrdom. Close your eyes and think of some things you are doing today that you don't want to do. Things you should do, but don't really want to do. Things you say to people that you don't really want to say. Explain to yourself such activities. What would happen if you did not do these things? What would you do instead? Tell your partner what you found out.

96. I Should...I Want. Each person in the circle says, "I should..." and finish the sentence. If the circle is large, one time around is enough. If the circle is small, you may want to go around the circle two or three times. Then, each person in the circle says, "I want..." and say what they want. One student, when asked, "How do you make yourself miserable?" answered, "I make a list of the things I want and throw it away. Then I make a list of what I should, and do it."

97. Sing a Song. In groups of four to six, each person in the group sings a song to the person on his right. Talk about your experience.

98. Be An Individual. All members walk around the group haphazardly, not touching or looking at anyone. Feel your individuality. After two minutes, continue walking, touching people's shoulders. (2 minutes) Continue walking, telling people, "Get out of my way!" push them, "Get!"

99. I See—I Imagine. Everyone gets a partner. Partners look at one another and each tells the other what he/she sees and then what they imagine about the other. Each talks five minutes, and after each has 5 minutes, they talk about what they learned.

100. Ball of Energy. (Myrna Haimowitz) Everyone stands in a circle. Leader has the ball of energy in right hand which quivers with energy. Leader shows how the ball of energy can make the hand move UP! and hand goes quickly toward the ceiling; or DOWN! and hand moves like a plummet to the floor; or BACK! and hand is pulled toward the rear; or LEFT! and hand goes to the left.

After leader demonstrates what the ball of energy can do, leader tells the group, "This energy can move, from the hand to the arm," (group watches and follows the leader, doing what the leader does), and from the arm to the shoulders, which become alive with movement, and down to the belly, and thighs and feet, and then back to the belly and shoulders and to the head and cheeks, and to the shoulders and arms and back to the hands.

Leader tells group, "Pass me the energy and I'll hold it while I explain the next step . . . I'll let the energy flow from one part of my body to another [vigorous demonstration] and then I'll throw the ball to you from one part of my body [from head, shoulders, belly, etc.] and you catch it in the same part of the body, let it move about and then throw the ball to someone else, until everyone has had a turn catching and throwing."

101. The Dawning of the Age of Aquarius. People lie in a star-shaped circle, their heads in the center and their feet pointing out, like rays from the sun. People are on their stomachs supported by their elbows. All close their eyes and say OMmmmmmmmmmm.

102. Massage from Parent, Massage from Child. Pick partners, and decide who's going to massage first. After this, no talking. Massager massages massagee first in a way he thinks she would like. Then the leader says to stop and massage in a way that feels good to the massager. This includes stopping when he wants to. Massager becomes massagee. (Feet or hands can be massaged, with or without massage lotion.) Repeat the instructions. When all the massagers are through, have partners tell each other what they noticed.

103. For Learning People's Names. (*Best for under twenty people.*) People sit in a circle. First person says her name. Next person says first person's name then her own name. Third person says first person's name, second person's name, then his name, and so on. It's O.K. to forget someone's name. If you forget, ask the person.

104. Description Game. (for people who know each other) One person leaves the room—he is "It" and has to guess whom the group has picked from among themselves. The only questions "It" can ask to help him guess the right person when he returns to the room is, "If this person were a _____ (animal, flower, season, muscial instrument, dessert, place, piece of furniture, TV show, etc.), what would they be?" Person who is guessing gets to ask one question like this of each person in the room, and gets three guesses.

105. I Should... (Clare Tutti) In pairs, X says to Y, "I should..." such as, "I should clean my house; I should get good grades; I should get a better job; I should come on time;" etc. and each time one says his *I should,* the other says, "Bullshit!" loudly. After a few minutes they switch—Y says to X, "I should..." and X says, "Bullshit!"

106. Secrets, and Myths About Secrets. (Muriel Adler) We have myths about secrets which prevent us from intimacy. "What will the neighbors think? Will my mother get sick if she finds out? No one will ever trust me with a secret again." Here is an exercise to get in touch with myths. (A) Close your eyes and think of the worst secrets that you have. (2 minutes) Think of what would happen if you told them to someone. (B) Open your eyes and write your secrets on a piece of paper and fold it up and throw it in the middle of the room (no names). (C) Each person in the group picks up one of the secrets and reads it aloud. (D) Discuss.

107. My Favorite Fairy Tale. Close your eyes. Imagine you are young again and think of who was your favorite comic strip, fairy tale, Biblical, radio or TV character. In small groups, pretend to be the person, telling how you dress, what you do, the kind of person you are. How are you like this today?

108. Forming a Temporary Family. In one-day or longer workshops, it may be helpful to begin with this exercise because it helps put strangers in touch with one another and get acquainted. The exercise takes 15 minutes to an hour.

A. Form an inner and outer circle, facing the center. Everyone in the outer circle turns to the right; the inner circle turns to the left. Rub the back of the person in front of you. (2 or 3 minutes) Walk in the circle, preferably to music, let yourself walk or dance to the music. Begin noticing the persons in the other circle who walk past you. (3 to 5 minutes)

B. Each male picks another male he would like as brother, and each female picks another female she would like to be her sister. Tell each other why you picked the other, what you like about them.

C. Each pair now picks two other pairs to form a family of six or eight people. Each family picks a father and mother. Each person in the family tells the family, "What I would like from you during this workshop..."

109. Handy Dandy Instant Joy. Ask someone who appears sad if they want to do an experiment called Handy Dandy Instant Joy. Tell the person: "Walk around the floor as though you are walking on your mother's new mattress. Feel the springiness. Bounce a little. Let yourself bounce more, and more. Imagine your mother comes into the room and says, 'STOP!' . . . And you say to your mother, as you continue to bounce, 'Hi, Mom, come join me! It's fun!' and she holds your hands while you bounce together." Others join, holding hands and jumping around.

110. Pornography as Seen by Different Ego States. (Muriel Adler) Everyone brings a piece of pornography to the group and shows it to a neighbor. They look at the pornography and describe what they see to each other with their Adult, then with their Child, and then with their Parent ego state.

111. The Most Powerful Sexual Experiences in My Life. (Steve Winners) Close your eyes and think of the most powerful sexual traumas in your life. How old were you when they occurred? What were you feeling? (3 to 5 minutes) Now think of the most positive sexual experiences you have had. (3 to 5 minutes) Open your eyes and look around the room. Think about why you wouldn't want to tell anyone about your experiences. Is it jealousy, shame, blackmail, that you fear? Often when people are abused sexually, they feel guilty. (3 minutes) Now tell your group about your experiences.

112. On Being the Other Sex. (Muriel Adler) Close your eyes and imagine you are a person of the other sex about 4 or 5 years old. What are you doing? How is your life different? (2 minutes) Now imagine you are 12 to 15 years old. What is happening to your body? How are you feeling? (3 minutes) You are grown up. Notice your body, your behavior, your feelings. (3 minutes) Open your eyes and discuss what you learned.

113. TA Rackets and the Muscles. Give a short lecture on rackets with examples of how they are lodged in the muscles: fear in the back of the neck; grief in the throat and chest, etc. The exercise demonstrates this theory.

All lie on the floor with plenty of space in between people. First tighten, then relax each of the sets of muscles to get in physical touch with the body. For example, "Stretch your right toe out as far as you can. Stretch it some more—tighter. Hold it. Now relax. Stretch your left heel out. Tighter. More. Relax. . . etc. Bend your right leg; tighten your buttocks; tighten your stomach; arch your back; scrunch up your shoulders; make a big smile; frown; stick out your tongue; raise your eyebrows; lower your eyebrows; tighten your fist; bring your right fist up tightly against your shoulder; stretch out your arm as far as it will go. . .etc.

"Now relax and think of some unfinished business you have with someone. Someone you are afraid of, or angry with, or wish to help. What would you like to say to that person or do with that person? Notice what is happening in your body as you have the fantasy. . .which muscles are getting involved?

"In groups of 3 or 4 tell what you found out."

114. Analysis of Obligated Time (Time that YOU feel is "obligated").
100% working hours
clients
boss
peers
friends
relatives
spouse/lover

children
plants/animals
agencies
house, farm, other
Total _____

Subtract the total from 100. This is time for yourself. "It's not that I don't love you. I love me too."

115. My Ability To Play. Analysis of play behavior through the eyes of others. How do you rate your ability to play?

-5	-4	-3	-2	-1	1	2	3	4	5

Very
Adaptive

Very
Playful

P: Peers   L: Lover   S: Subordinate   I: You
B: Boss   C: Children   M: Mother
F: Friends   G: Group   D: Father

WHO sees you play best?

116. What's Important. (a) In pairs, tell your partner as the parent of your opposite sex what is important in life. The partner is a little "you." (For example, be your mother and tell your partner what is important in life. (b) Be the parent of the same sex and tell a friend what you do for fun.

117. What I Want. In pairs, one person be all Child, saying everything he wants as fast as his mouth can say them. The other person be adaptive, realistic. Switch.

118. Getting Married In 3 Minutes. Teacher tells everyone to stand in two circles, one inside the other, the inside circle walking clockwise, the outside circle walking the other way. Everyone looks at everyone else. Let the circles fall apart and people walk around looking at each other. In three minutes you will all be married. Find someone to marry and sit down. When everyone is married, talk about what you think will be the strengths of your marriage and what will be the areas of conflict. How will you resolve the conflicts? Take about five minutes. Then married couples get into groups of six persons (3 couples) and continue the discussion.

119. My Family. Draw a picture of you and your family doing something together when you were little. Discuss what you learned with the group.

120. Strengths and Accomplishments. Interview your partner and find out what his strengths and accomplishments are. Take about 3 minutes for each. Now introduce your partner to the group and tell what his strengths and accomplishments are.

121. Most Precious to Me. Get five little slips of paper. Write down on each slip one thing that you most value, that is most precious to you, so when you have finished, you have five slips with five different most precious or valuable things to you. Now I will come around and pick up one slip. Give me the one of the five that you could most easily do without. (Teacher picks up one slip from each person.) Now I will come pick up the next most precious (does this until each person has only one slip left). Tell your partner what you did, what you found out, how you will nurture what is most precious to you.

122. Making Contact and Avoiding Contact. Half the group lines up on one side of the room. The other half lines up on the other side. Those to the teacher's right walk over to someone they are interested in on the other side and work at making contact. Anything goes except hurting or sex. Those on the teacher's left work at avoiding contact. After five minutes the two persons switch, so that those who were avoiding contact are now working at making contact. Tell each other what you learned.

123. Art Therapy Exercises. (Jeanne Wiger) Materials needed: paper, crayons or paints. Imagine you are little, maybe 3 years or 4 years old. Shut your eyes and get in touch with yourself, go back and become very young. What do you remember? What is going on around you? Take one of the colors that represents what you are feeling and fill in the sheet of paper with that color. (Pause 3 or 4 minutes.) Now come back and be the age you are now. Think of the world you left. Get in touch with the feelings you had in your life today and how you feel about yourself and the world around you. Are you happy, sad, scared or angry? Imagine you are becoming younger and younger. Get into your drawing that you just created. Where are you? How does it feel to be there? Begin to explore that world. What does it mean in your life today? Get into groups of two or three and tell each other what you found out.

124. Broken Record—or Repeat Repeat. Your neighbor has borrowed your lawn mower and your lawn is getting 10" high, and you want to cut it today, on your day off. You phone your neighbor and ask him to return it to you today. He is reluctant, says he is busy, will do it tomorrow or next week. You answer each of his arguments accepting his point of view, and each time you add, "I want it back today." Divide into groups of three. "A" wants his lawn mower back, "B" says no, and "C" helps "A."

125. Feelings Toward Visiting and Invading. (Jeanne Wiger) Materials needed: construction paper, crayons or magic markers. A large group may be divided into groups of 2, 3 or 4 persons. All participants in the small groups share the same sheet of paper. Instructions: Each person selects a portion of the paper to be his territory, making a picture on it, with the left hand, or non-dominant hand, sharing crayons or paints. After 5 or 10 minutes, participants are invited to continue their pictures, but to enlarge them and enter into the territories of the others in the group. After 10 minutes participants discuss their reactions.

126. An Exercise to Relate Physical Tension to a Possible Racket. See section *Rackets and the Human Body.*

127. Changing a Recurrent Dream, or a Way of Thinking Using Senoi Techniques.

Helen: (recurring dream) I am going over a bridge, and I can't help it, but I crash into the side of it.

Therapist: And when you are awake?

Helen: I'm scared of crossing bridges.

Therapist: It's your dream. You can change it any way you like. You are in charge of your dreams. Do you like the dream?

Helen: No, it's scary.

Therapist: Talk to the spirit of the bridge, a very powerful spirit.

Helen: I'm scared.

Therapist: Yes, you are very brave to face such a powerful spirit alone. Close your eyes and imagine someone is there to help you. You can bring anyone you want to help you since it's your dream. Who would you like to help you?

Helen: My grandma. Grandma, will you help me? Grandma says sure. She is with me.

Therapist: Talk to the bridge . . . What does the bridge answer?

Helen: You will ride across me and die.

Therapist: You like that reply?

Helen: No.

Therapist: You are not a victim of circumstance. You create your own dream. What do you want the spirit of the bridge to say?

Helen: The bridge says, die, die.

Therapist: Ask the bridge what he needs to be your friend. } This sequence repeated three times.

Helen: What do you want from me?

Bridge: I want you to look at me, to talk to me, look at me.

Helen: (exasperated, to Therapist) I only said that because I know you wanted me to.

Therapist: How do you like what the bridge said?

Helen: Ok, that's ok, I'll look, I'll look. (she frequently does not look at people)

The following week she reported looking at bridges, noticing the details of their construction, their image against sky and trees, with curiosity and without fear. We had a no-suicide contract earlier. What this work does is help Helen to realize she can change her thoughts. Berne said, "I'm a head mechanic." This is an example of head mechanics.

106